NELLY DON: A STITCH

COMPANION TO THE FILM *NELLY DON: A STITCH IN TIME*

Terence Michael O'Malley

LIMITED EDITION

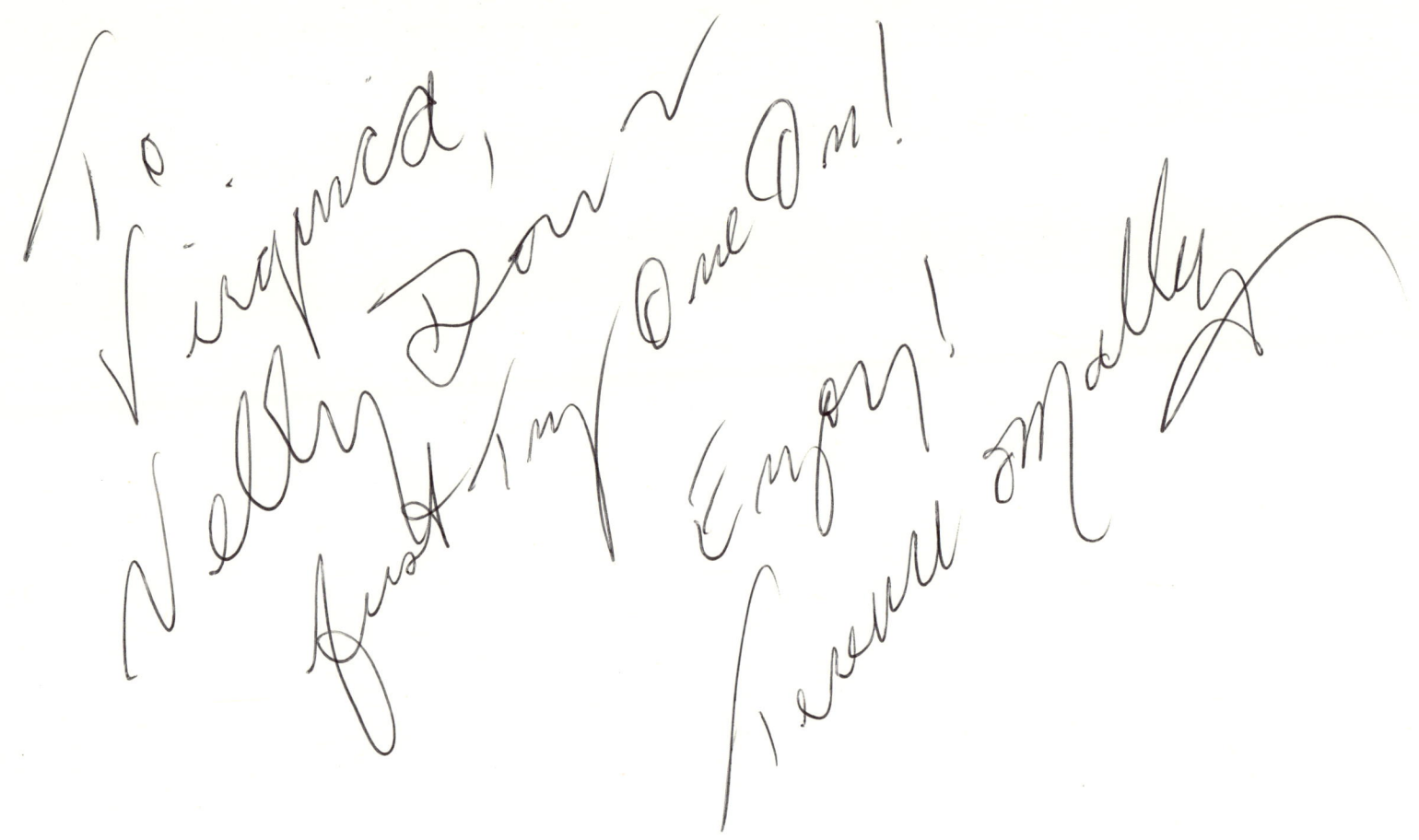

© Copyright 2006 by Terence Michael O'Malley

All rights reserved. No part of this book may be reproduced, stored in a retrieval system,
or transmitted in any form or by any means, electronic, mechanical, photocopying, recording or otherwise,
without prior consent of the copyright holder.

First Edition

Printing and Production, J. Audley, The Covington Group
Book design by Randy Lackey, The Covington Group
Website (back cover) design by Kevin Fox
Manufactured by The Covington Group, Inc.

ISBN: 1-59971-017-X

Table of Contents

1. **NELLY DON COLLAGE OF FASHION THROUGH THE DECADES** 1

2. **NBC RADIO DRAMATIZES NELLY DON IN THE GOLDEN NEEDLE** ... 22
   - How it all began
   - A modern business romance
   - Peck's takes a chance
   - An empire is born

3. **FROM COUNTY CORK, IRELAND, TO JACKSON COUNTY, MO** 26
   - The old sod
   - Beginning life in Parsons
   - The move to KC
   - A young bride
   - Learning at Lindenwood
   - Time to keep house
   - The apron string kept stretching

4. **WE'RE IN THE MONEY!** 30
   - Nelly Don: Just Try One On
   - Like a fairy tale come true

5. **THE OLDER THE FIDDLE THE SWEETER THE TUNE** 36
   - Paul dissipates
   - Hello James A. Reed
   - A scandalous affair
   - Reed to Truman – two degrees of separation
   - Reed to the rescue
   - Murder by poison
   - The League of Nations is a colossal fraud
   - Reed for president

6. **HANDY DANDY TO THE RESCUE** 47
   - Nell at leisure

7. **DAVID QUINLAN DONNELLY** 50
   - Nell delivers an adopted child

8. **KIDNAPPING** 52
   - Beat her! Hit her on the head!
   - Cheap cottage cots
   - Reed to the rescue
   - Mob boss Johnny Lazia feels the heat!
   - A fine big car!
   - Nell posts an award
   - The bigamist heads to South Africa
   - Justice is served

9. **GOODBYE PAUL DONNELLY** 61
   - The 1.27 million dollar divorce
   - Pendergast loyal to Reed to the end
   - Surprise, we're married!
   - Paul Donnelly suffers a tormented death

10. **NELL THE BENEFICENT EXECUTIVE** 65
    - Nell, Reed and David – A happy family!
    - Hardwood floors
    - Air conditioning
    - Pension plan
    - Employee scholarships
    - Remnants and slightly damaged store
    - Lemonade cart
    - The mansion
    - The farm
    - On-site medical
    - Merry Christmas!

11. **UNION TARGET: NELLY DON** 69
    - Reed assails The New Deal
    - FDR retaliates
    - A long, legal battle
    - Of course Nell wins, she's Nell!

12. **NELLY DON GOES TO WAR** 71
    - Fashions to kill
    - Rosie the Riveter's clothier
    - The fighting senator succumbs

13. **NELLY DON AT ITS ZENITH!** 76
    - A fashion parade, 1940s, 1950s, 1960s
    - The houses of Nelly Don
    - Radio ad copy

14. **NELL DEVOTES HERSELF TO ALTRUISM** 85
    - Boards and commissions
    - The wildlife and recreation area
    - George Blair: loyal friend and confidante
    - Nelly Don files for bankruptcy
    - Nell the republican
    - Nell bags a buck
    - Nell: The grande dame of the garment industry

Special acknowledgements:

The Independent – Nelly Don Ad p. 32

Jackson County Historical Society – Fashions in Kansas City Ad p. 78

From the "Goin' To Kansas City Collection" courtesy of The Kansas
City Star and the Kansas City Museum/Union Station – Johnny Lazia photo p. 55

Lindenwood College – 1909 Linden Leaves Yearbook photos p. 29

Western Historical Manuscript Collection, Kansas City, Missouri – Golden Needle Poster and
Photograph of Pecks pp. 22 and 23

Wichita State University Libraries: Department of Special Collections – Postcard of Parsons p. 27

Wilborn and Associates – Kansas City Postcard p. 28

Introduction

Nelly Don: A Stitch in Time
Companion to the documentary film *Nelly Don: A Stitch in Time*
by Terence Michael O'Malley

This book is an afterthought, a complete impulse, encouraged by a few persons who understand that Nelly Don merits a book. Its purpose is to complement the film with images and story lines that offer extra insight into these extraordinary people.

Nelly Don was the largest dress manufacturer's label in America for more than 50 years from 1916 to 1978. But Nelly Don was also a captivating woman, who inverted her last name (Donnelly) to found what would become a fashion empire, making 5,000 dresses a day.

It's the cavalcade of 20th century styles that makes this project naturally visual. One sees women's fashions change and appreciates Nell's profound influence on how millions of American women attired themselves. Women trusted her because she had an affordable flair for fashion.

Nell's accomplishments are all the more astounding considering the eras of her lifespan. Born first-generation American-Irish in 1889, the 12th of 13 children, she left her Parsons, Kansas, home at age 16 to live in a boardinghouse in Kansas City. She wed at age 17, went to college at 19 and made her first million dollars by age 27, reinventing the Housedress.

Nell's personal travails are nothing short of gripping. Her first husband became a besotted lecher, the depression threatened her workers, she wanted a baby but was already 40 years old, the Senator was so enthralling and her kidnapping was terrorizing. Heroic Kansas City gangsters had to rescue her.

The International Ladies Garment Workers Union targeted Nelly Don, but her workers signed a loyalty pact rejecting outside agitators. During WWII, Nell made 5 million pairs of GI underwear, but refused to be a war profiteer. In 1947, she built the largest dress manufacturing plant in the world, spanning two city blocks. The story remains fabled right up to her death.

This book (and the documentary) are blessed by access to the David Quinlan Reed family archives. By way of full disclosure, Nell is my great, great aunt (making me a pretty, pretty good nephew). Mary Quinlan McCormick, Nell's eldest sibling, is my great grandmother. Nell is just three years older than her niece, Kate (McCormick) Baty, my grandmother. She and my grandmother grew up like sisters and were lifelong friends. My mother was very much a favored niece of Nell and thus it is with great honor that I present Nell's story to you.

This book is dedicated to my wife, Heather, whose support and affection I cherish most.

Heather O'Malley (left) dining with Tinker Reed, 2005.

Chapter One

Nelly Don: Collage of Fashion Through the Decades

To begin the book I have chosen fashion images in order by decade, because in the final analysis the dresses are Nell's most enduring legacy. Nell made frocks and dresses purchased by millions of moms, aunts, grandmothers, sisters and daughters across a wide range of socio-economic classes. There are two major reasons why Nell was the most important clothier for women in the 20th century: quality and affordability.

As you peruse the fashion collage on these next 20 pages, look at the dress design in conjunction with its utility. I say utility not to demean the fashions as being work clothes. Rather, the dresses work for women. Most Nelly Dons had extra hemline, waistline, adjustable shoulder straps, movable belt loops and always a pocket somewhere on the garment, a hallmark of Nelly Don design.

The benefit of choosing the Nelly Don story as both a film and book is its inherent visual quality. Had Nell chosen some other type of industry, perhaps her story would not be so enchanting. But because her life's mission was to champion the beauty of women through clothing, her story is like candy for the eyes, happy, pleasing – both sensual and wholesomely delicious. Nell was a maven for advertising, publicity and promotion, leaving behind a trove of circulars, pamphlets, miniature books, magazine articles and two 16 mm industrial films. The "House of Nelly Don" film (1936) has Nell's stamp all over it by starting with The William Tell Overture (her favorite music was classical) and including that snappy tune, Ave Maria.

Nell adopted the persona of "Nelly Don" and actually was addressed and introduced within the fashion and manufacturing industries as Nelly Don, so that every time her name

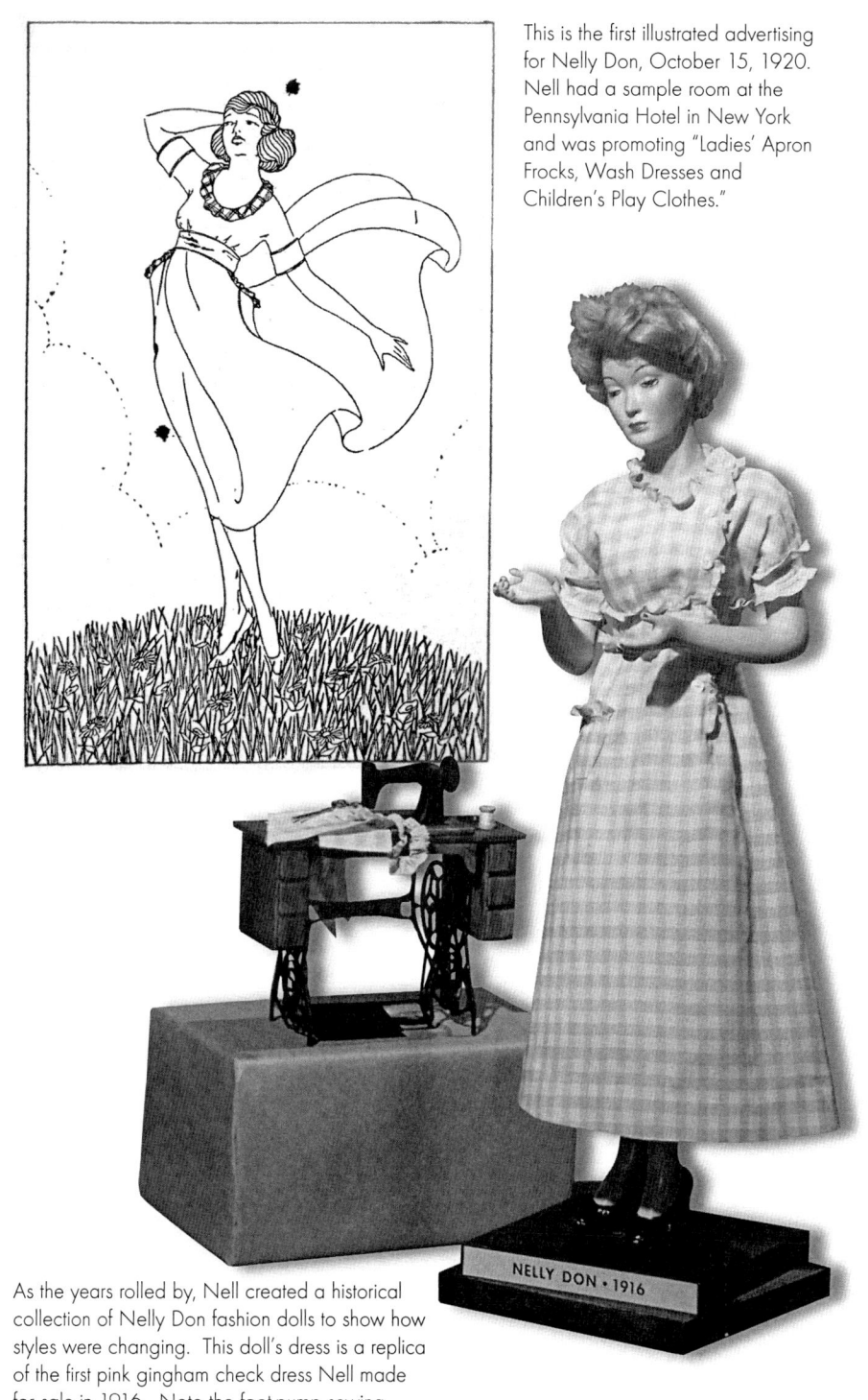

This is the first illustrated advertising for Nelly Don, October 15, 1920. Nell had a sample room at the Pennsylvania Hotel in New York and was promoting "Ladies' Apron Frocks, Wash Dresses and Children's Play Clothes."

As the years rolled by, Nell created a historical collection of Nelly Don fashion dolls to show how styles were changing. This doll's dress is a replica of the first pink gingham check dress Nell made for sale in 1916. Note the foot-pump sewing machine used in those days.

was spoken her dresses were promoted as well. Nell understood every aspect of her business, not just the design. Her first husband, Paul Donnelly (about whom very little is known), was a former credit manager at Barton Brothers Shoe Company. He ran the business side of the Donnelly Garment Company (Nelly Don was the trade name for the dresses). Nell directed her energies toward not only fashion design, but also how the textile industry worked and how to apply European silk designs to cotton and rayon for American dresses. Nell traveled by steamship to Europe on many occasions and brought home with her ideas of how to make her dresses rival those of the latest fashions of Paris and Vienna.

What is interesting is that the original pink gingham check frock that sold so wildly in 1916 at Peck's Dry Goods Store in Kansas City was really quite humble. As historian Jane Flynn wryly noted, "It makes you wonder what in the world it replaced." And that's a problem because the Mother Hubbard dresses that Nell ultimately refused to wear have not survived as artifacts and were not widely advertised or depicted visually. The dresses promoted in the first 15 years of the 20th century were high fashions, clothing a woman would wear out shopping or to church or some other public locale. But the common, everyday housedress that a woman toiled in during the week did not require much promotion and was widely available at dry goods stores off the rack in calico cloth for 69 cents.

Nell told the Nelly Don story fundamentally the same way with a few minor inconsistencies leaving some detail unanswered. Was the first Peck's buyer a man or a woman? Did Peck's sell a few sample dresses first, then order 18 dozen from her? Was the business begun in her attic or living room? What is known without question is that throughout her forty years with the company, originality was her key pitch and she kept pace with every change in vogue.

To get the company running, Nell speculated by purchasing used foot-pump sewing machines, so upon her first order she was ready to go. As more orders came in she realized that she needed greater, more efficient output so she turned to the aviation and car manufacturing industries and

Continued on Page 7

Anna Ruth Donnelly, Paul Donnelly's sister, was the first "model" for Nelly Don, wearing the pink gingham check frock that was a best seller.

This dress is depicted on an advertising brochure for the store Woodward & Lothrop in Washington, D.C. "Exquisite in every detail is this Floral Print Frock with appliqué trim. Selected from our Nelly Dons at $3.95" (c. 1928)

Nell was great at cross-promotion as seen here in this newspaper ad (c. 1926) where Nelly Don frocks are "worn by the ushers."

Another Woodward & Lothrop dress depicted as part of their Nelly Don Spring Fashions. "An impressive value is this chic Donelin Print Frock."

Nelly Don: Collage of Fashion Through the Decades

The cut line for this print ad reads: "Tis inward satisfaction to don a Nelly Don." (c. 1926)

Another doll from the historical Nelly Don collection shows the emphasis placed on ruffles and accessories like buttons, pockets and bows in 1919.

These "drop waist" fashions popular in the 1920s were ankle-length linens designed for wear at all informal daytime occasions.

This is an advertising circular from the Summer of 1929. Nell still refers to her dresses as "frocks," a term that is now out of vogue. Note the prices of $2.98 per frock.

One of several beautiful prints for consumption overseas, the series depicts the evolution of Nelly Don fashions from the 1920s to the 1940s.

She Put A Million Wives Into Pretty Clothes

Nelly Don Proved Lovely Bright-Colored Frocks as Practical as the Old-Fashioned Drab Ones

NEW YORK, N.Y.—Nelly Don hated drab house dresses. So she made gay ones—only a few at first. They sold amazingly. Now her business totals $2,000,000 a year.

In spite of hard wear, they are practical, she finds. Because with modern Lux cleansing they wear and wear!

"The very best way to wash the lovely, bright colored materials we use," Nelly Don says, "is with Lux. Lux has no harmful alkali and with Lux there is no rubbing.

NELLY DON

No matter how delicate a color or pattern, it can be washed in Lux time after time—often for years—and still look just like new."

Nell was the subject of many newspaper and magazine articles over the years. Her astounding success by 1929, about the time this article appeared, was already the stuff of legend.

Nelly Don: Collage of Fashion Through the Decades

"Frost Brothers Institution of Fashion" in San Antonio sold Nelly Don Frocks in the late 1930s. In a paroxysm of vernal exuberance, the narrative reads: "One look and we could almost see robins hopping by, crocuses in bloom!"

Nelly Don changed with the seasons, giving endless reasons for a woman to expand her wardrobe. This dress is from a circular whereby a person could mail order a dress. (c. 1935)

By the late 1930s, Nell made her dresses in rayons, silks, linens and cottons creating the "cleverest lines" of dresses and the "most flattering color-effects for your opening bow to Spring."

This 1939 Salesgram encouraged saleswomen to "Sell Yourself," by wearing smart Nelly Don dresses with slide fasteners and adjustable waistlines with a "new type of belt loop which can slide twice the length of the belt width giving wide adjustability."

Nell believed in giving a face to her dress line creating an alter ego for herself, Nelly Don. In private, among family and friends she was known simply as Nell.

In 1939, Nell announced a "label change," whereupon "Nelly Don now places her label over the size and style number on dresses $7.95 and up...giving a trimmer appearance to the inside back neckline as you present the dress to your customer."

Fall is an imaginative creature . . . colorful and changing in itself, it inspires its beholders to color and change as well.

Fall is a perennial "renaissance"—bringing with it a new zest for living, for making new plans, selecting new clothes.

We believe our new Nelly Don styles have captured the charm and spirit, the beauty and color of this season. They are smart, versatile styles, matching the lives of the American women for whom they were designed . . . ready now to become a part of those busy lives . . . to work, to play, to go to school—to fit American budgets as well as American plans!

Nelly Don

Nell understood that women love fashion shows and virtually every Nelly Don function included a fashion show of some sort. Nell also liked to promote how well her clothes washed, i.e., "easily tubbed."

Continued from Page 2

applied section production principles to dress making. Before Nell came along, American women would order fashion dresses to be tailored individually. Nell approached it differently by manufacturing stylish dresses in multiple sizes to fit a broad spectrum of feminine shapes.

The key to Nelly Don's exceptional growth as a dress line came in the early 1920s, when the simple housedress emerged from its domesticity and was seen on the streets at large. There were morning frocks, afternoon dresses, sports frocks, school apparel, business dress, vacation togs and fashions for every informal occasion.

Nell steered the company through the Great Depression and World War II with resounding success. She sold her interest in the Donnelly Garment Company in 1956 at age 67; 40 years after it began and about 38 years after she made her first million dollars.

"Watch these trends as the season unfolds. The craze for gold – gold detail on belts, pockets, necklines ... most Nelly Don trims, by the way, are detachable."

In the early 1940s, Nell introduced "Playtonics, play clothes for casual living." Playtonics was a new name for new versions of original favorites, Donsembles, Donabouts and Don-Alls. These skirts, culottes and overalls were remarkably versatile. For instance, the removable skirt could be used as a shawl or blanket. But the Playtonics line may have been ahead of its time, and with the onset of WWII, it was phased out after only a few years.

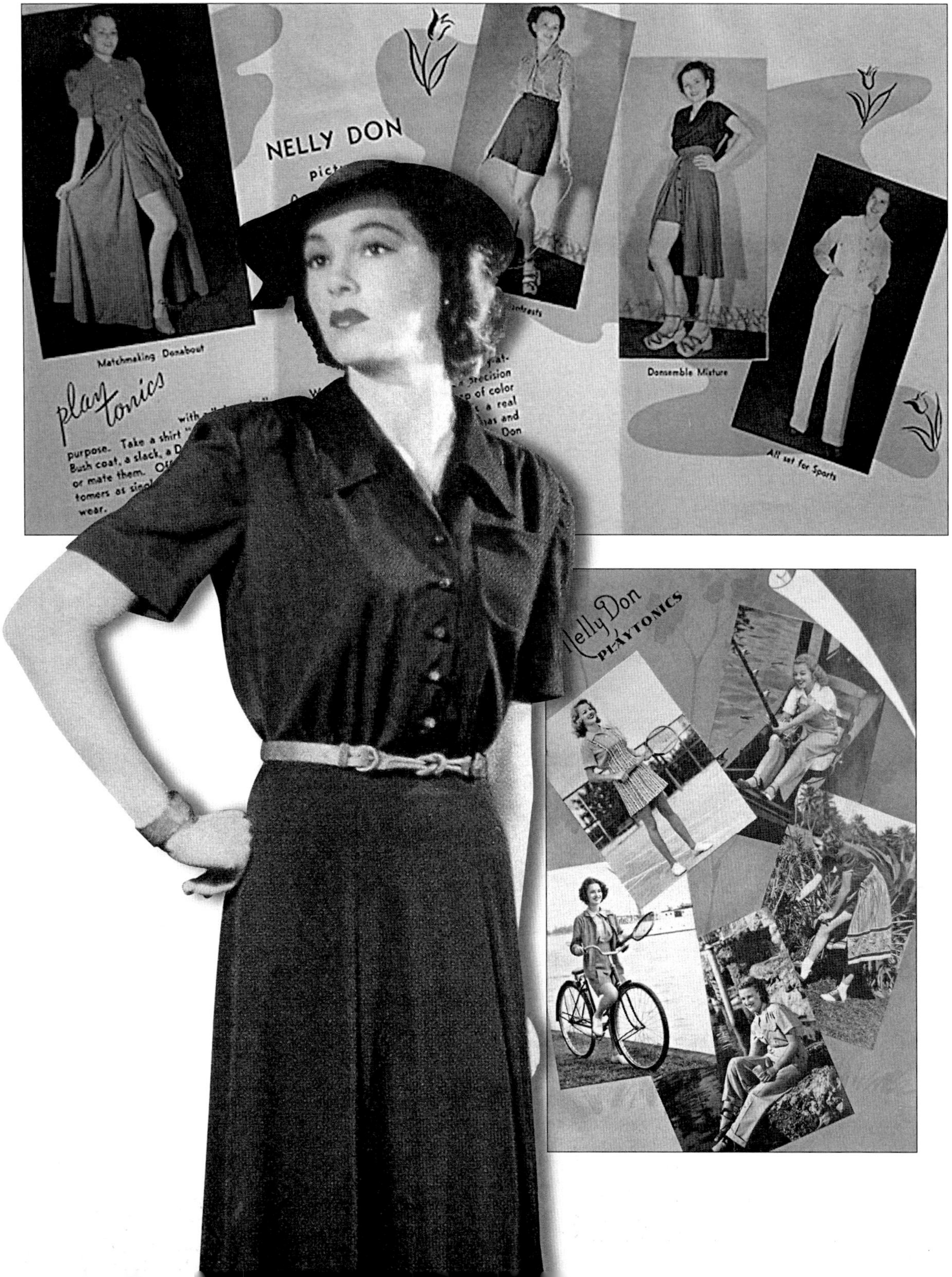
NELLY DON
Matchmaking Donabout
playtonics
Donsemble Mixture
All set for Sports
Nelly Don
PLAYTONICS

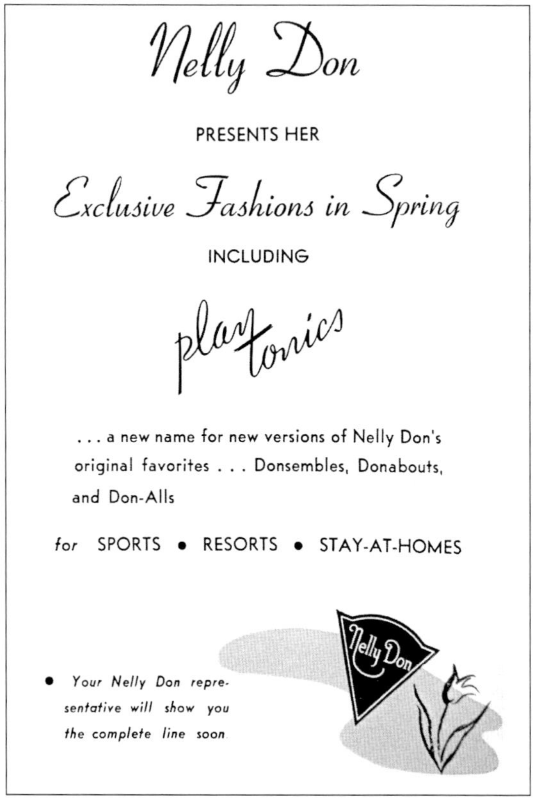
Nelly Don
PRESENTS HER
Exclusive Fashions in Spring
INCLUDING
playtonics
. . . a new name for new versions of Nelly Don's original favorites . . . Donsembles, Donabouts, and Don-Alls
for SPORTS • RESORTS • STAY-AT-HOMES
• Your Nelly Don representative will show you the complete line soon
Nelly Don

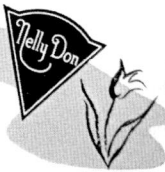

Nelly Don: Collage of Fashion Through the Decades

"Nelly Don Shantung Sheer (spun rayon), famous spring-spirited fabric, takes to graceful, feminine lines. Exclusive flower cluster print Soapsuds Fashion" is how Nell promoted this dress in 1940.

"Spike its smart simplicity with jewelry accents," was one way of gussying up a Nelly Don, such as this 1940s plaid cotton ensemble.

Nelly Don Size Chart

Realizing that many women had imperfect figures, Nell designed her dresses for virtually any size woman, long waisted, trim waisted, full figure, short waisted and so forth.

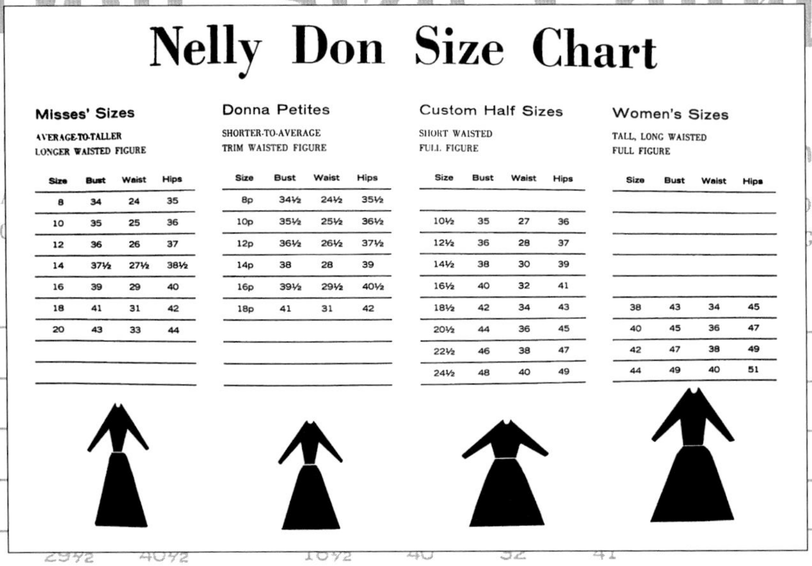

Misses' Sizes
AVERAGE-TO-TALLER
LONGER WAISTED FIGURE

Size	Bust	Waist	Hips
8	34	24	35
10	35	25	36
12	36	26	37
14	37½	27½	38½
16	39	29	40
18	41	31	42
20	43	33	44

Donna Petites
SHORTER-TO-AVERAGE
TRIM WAISTED FIGURE

Size	Bust	Waist	Hips
8p	34½	24½	35½
10p	35½	25½	36½
12p	36½	26½	37½
14p	38	28	39
16p	39½	29½	40½
18p	41	31	42

Custom Half Sizes
SHORT WAISTED
FULL FIGURE

Size	Bust	Waist	Hips
10½	35	27	36
12½	36	28	37
14½	38	30	39
16½	40	32	41
18½	42	34	43
20½	44	36	45
22½	46	38	47
24½	48	40	49

Women's Sizes
TALL, LONG WAISTED
FULL FIGURE

Size	Bust	Waist	Hips
38	43	34	45
40	45	36	47
42	47	38	49
44	49	40	51

848—New design in Strato Sheer rayon that's all flattery to all women! Tailored softly, ingeniously, with tucks in long, graceful lines from shoulder to hem. Navy, Spring brown, black. 12.44.

Nelly Don Anniversary Stars ★ 5.00

For Nelly Don Week only, January 6-12! Special values at a special price, for as long as we have them in stock this week! Famous Nelletta Sheers (washable Enka rayon) to choose early, and wear endlessly . . . to slip you smoothly round the clock and straight through the calendar!

★ 1632—Forever young, forever new . . . Spring polka dots in a Nelly Don design that keeps its femininity with its nicely tailored lines! In sapphire, black, wine, rust. 14-40. $5.00.

★ Top, 1630—Shirring detail accents youthful lines, while print adds color to dark accessories. Blue, Java brown, turquoise, rose. 12-40. $5.00.

★ Right, 1631—At once pretty and practical, with easy lines from the softly gathered neckline to flared hem. In rose, navy, Bahama blue, green. 14-44. $5.00.

Nelly Don: Collage of Fashion Through the Decades

All the fashions on this page are from the early 1940s. Nell's infectious enthusiasm for pretty clothes permeates her advertising: "Your colors are sun-filtered rays of gold and lime, romantic shades of pink and blue. Your plans are many, busy hours at home, or shopping, traveling to a chosen spot. Your gay accomplice is NELLY DON who'll dress you in the height of Soapsuds Fashion."

FALL right in with Nelly Don's Autumn proposals. Burnished colors with a bent to subtle accents that give zest to your costume.

The Deep South inspired these dresses released on Nelly Don's Silver Anniversary in 1941. "The beauty of its landscapes, the color and enchantment of its famous gardens have been captured in her prints and styles."

Nelly Don: Collage of Fashion Through the Decades

13

Nell resumed designing sharp dresses for women after WWII. Waistlines were smaller, but as the picture with two models suggests, the same dress could complement different body shapes. One fashion accessory most women likely do not miss is the "blushing veil" attached to women's hats.

Nelly Don - Spring '53 Wardrobe Ideas

1953: Nelly Don is the largest dress manufacturer in the world. Her dresses were sold in every major market in America and many countries overseas.

Nelly Don: Collage of Fashion Through the Decades

Soft-tailor suit in new ribbed menswear suiting of rayon and acetate, crease-resistant. Red, grey, rust. 12 to 40 and 12½ to 20½.

The 1950s for Nelly Don were high fashion, although her lines were never intended as formal evening wear. Nelly Dons were famous for fit and how well they were made notwithstanding their mass production. Customers were advised: "Nelly Dons are cut on full standard measurements like the most expensive dress you own. Nothing spared to give good lines. Please don't overestimate your size in ordering."

McCreery's in New York City; Carson, Pirie, Scott in Chicago; Shillito's of Cincinnati; Goldwater's in Phoenix; and, Rich's of Atlanta all carried Nelly Dons during the 1950s. Nelly Don provided radio spot announcements for retailers: "And Nelly Don, you know, is the designer who believes that every woman can look like a million without spending one. Stop in today and 'Just Try One On.'"

Most Nelly Don dresses could be washed and drip-dried with minimum ironing. "Here are the looks you'll love for Fall. Designed by Nelly Don to give you more smart fashion per hour...anytime, anywhere your plans take you."

NELLY DON: A Stitch In Time

Promotional copy: "The first bright looks of the new season, in beautifully made fashions to take you from here to Spring. Completely feminine fashions with the pretty look in fluid silhouettes and carefree fabrics, plus the careful attention to fit and quality dressmaking you expect from Nelly Don."

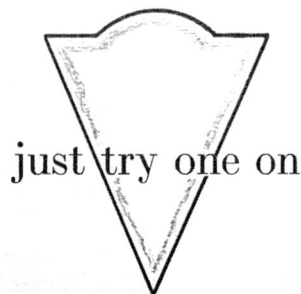

The 1960s.

Nelly Don: Collage of Fashion Through the Decades

Shadow-dot chiffon, slimming skirt banded with tucks, embroidered sheath, sun striped shirtdress are how the four dresses at the top of this page are described from left to right. Nelly Don radio ad copy: "Nelly Don casts cool shadows on the Summer scene with a collection of smart new fashions in dark town tones."

Promotional copy: "The well-dressed woman demands both fashion and quality in her wardrobe. Nelly Don selects the finest fabrics, gives you excellent cut and fit, and pays careful attention to dressmaker touches and finishing details...and she brings them to you at sensible prices."

Nelly Don: Collage of Fashion Through the Decades

The 1960s.

Promotional copy: "Double-stitching at the waistline tape in one-piece dresses. Rip out the top row of stitching for added shoulder-to-waist length. Winter-weary wardrobes welcome a bright new look and you'll find our favorite fashion look in this collection. Slender sheath lines, softly pleated skirts, superb double-knit cottons, new textured blends and of course every Nelly Don features the excellent cut, fit and detailing that have made her a favorite American designer."

Chapter Two

NBC Radio Dramatizes Nelly Don in The Golden Needle

Being the stuff of legend, Nell's story garnered the attention of the NBC (Radio) Network, producer of "The Cavalcade of America" radio program. On January 17, 1950, NBC broadcast to a national radio audience of 8 million listeners "The Golden Needle: The Story of Nelly Don," starring actress Dorothy McGuire who just two years prior was nominated for an Academy Award as best actress in the film "Gentleman's Agreement."

The production values of the hour-long radio program are solid, but the writing and story lines are sappy and gushy. Paul Donnelly, Nell's first husband to whom she was married for 26 years, is never mentioned and the story skips Nell's kidnapping. Still, not many people have their lives dramatized before the rest of the country, underscoring the narrative quality of Nell's life.

This chapter allows you to read in Nell's own words how Nelly Don came to be. In 1926, Nell published "A Modern Business Romance," a booklet celebrating the Nelly Don story and commending Paul Donnelly as being a selfless husband who supported his wife's endeavors without reservation. That was pretty good spin considering their relationship deteriorated in truth.

In many articles, Nell gives a lot of credit to Paul for the initial success of Nelly Don. In 1916, Paul put up the $1,270 Nell needed to capitalize that first big order from Peck's (18 dozen dresses). When America entered World War I, 34 year-old Paul Donnelly enlisted in the army and went to officers training camp. But before he left, he secured for Nell a line of credit and obtained factory space. While Paul was serving his country, Nell was busy making him a very wealthy man.

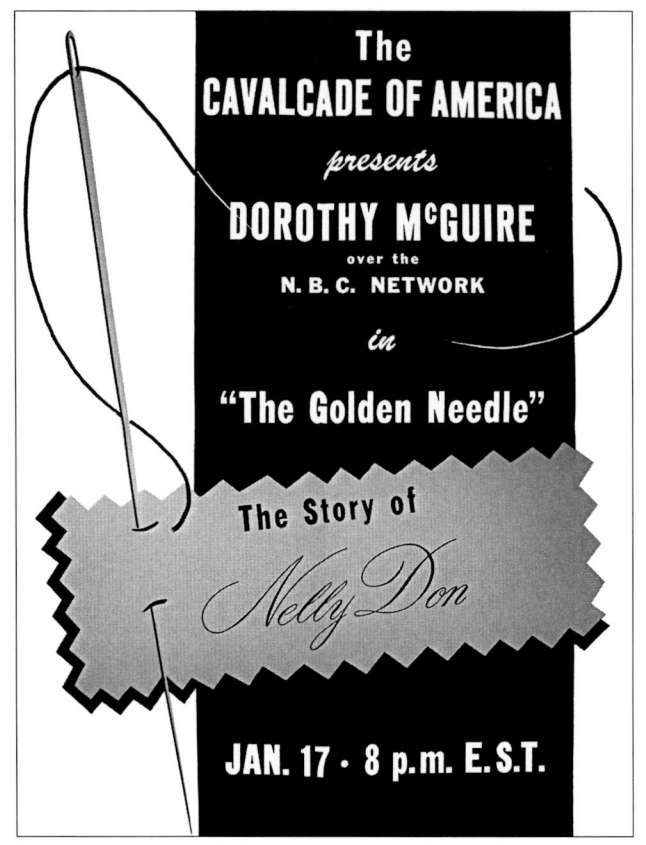

DuPont, "makers of better living through chemistry," sponsored the 1950 radio program "The Golden Needle" dramatizing Nell's life. The poster was used to promote the program. Academy Award nominee Dorothy McGuire portrayed Nell in the radio program. Two days after its broadcast, McGuire sent a telegram to Nell saying it was "great fun playing 'quote you.'"

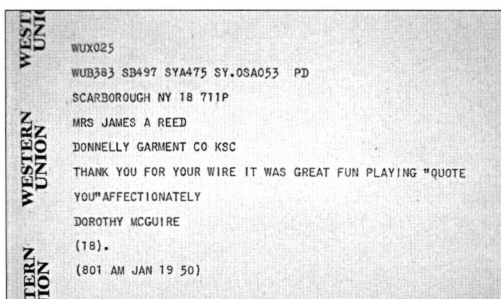

Dorothy McGuire stars in the "Cavalcade of America" play on NBC Tuesday at 8 P. M.

NBC Radio Dramatizes Nelly Don in The Golden Needle

TWENTY YEARS FORWARD!

• From a small house a large one grew through twenty years . . . adhering now as always to the ideal that there is no substitute for quality.

• From 1 to 20 years—from 2 employees to 1249 employees.

• Back in 1916 Nelly Don began it all. Beginning with two workers she completed the first year with a total payroll of $2,500.

• And then it grew until in 1929 there were 875 persons in the Nelly Don family.

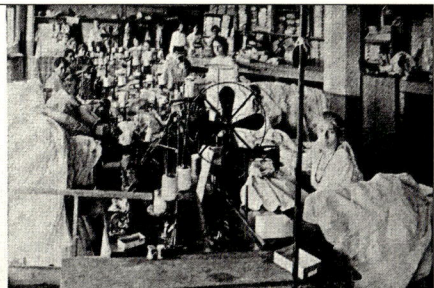

Nelly Don Factory in 1919 with 18 employees.

• And each year it grew . . . in 1935 the Nelly Don house sheltered 1175 employees with a payroll for the year of $1,469,000. On into 1936—and the House that Nelly Don Built continues its growth.

Page Seven

Nell published the booklet "A Modern Business Romance" in 1926, offering a saccharine version of how Nelly Don began and how her first husband, Paul Donnelly, was responsible for its success.

At far left is an excerpt from another small booklet published in 1936 called *Fashions To Live In* from The House that Nelly Don Built (see page 65).

At bottom right is a photo of 12th and Main Streets in Kansas City (c. 1913). Partly obscured is the sign for PECK'S, the dry goods store that ordered the first 18 dozen Nelly Don dresses.

A MODERN BUSINESS ROMANCE

How a young housewife found a million dollar business at the end of her apron string.   :-:   :-:   :-:

Copyright 1926
Donnelly Garment Co.
Kansas City, Mo.

NELLY DON
(Mrs. Paul F. Donnelly)

How It All Began

DISCONTENT . . and a Slim Purse . . . rather unromantic factors to play leading roles in a romance—really started it all. A woman's dissatisfaction with her clothes usually starts something far different, but in the case of Nell Donnelly it started a "tale of exciting adventures" . . . one of Webster's ways of saying *a romance*.

Nell Donnelly was a bride—youthful, vivacious—fond of pretty clothes, as all brides are. Keeping house was to her a new and exciting adventure, and her dramatic, artistic instinct impelled her to dress her part. Half the fun would be to have a pretty kitchen—the ambition of every bride—and to be the prettiest picture in it.

Had her purse been unlimited, this tale might never have been written,

Then Her Big Idea Was Born

FRIENDS had convinced her that women really wanted pretty home frocks. They longed for the kind she made—they liked the colors she liked. They were tired and discouraged with the ugly, drab "sixty-nine cent creations" made of flimsy, dreary looking materials, that were hastily thrown together.

Women simply couldn't buy the kind of frocks they wanted. This she knew because she had tried. Many mothers didn't have time to make their own dresses, others couldn't sew, and thousands of housewives like herself couldn't pay high prices for frocks that, though they might be better in quality, were no prettier than the cheap garments of servitude.

And then the thought came. Could she—why shouldn't she make frocks that stores would buy to sell to their customers who wanted just the kind of frocks she and her friends and relatives wanted. Why not try... *and she did.*

Nelly Don Went "A-Selling"

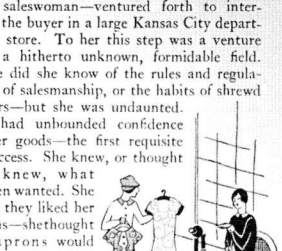

WITH a few crisp, colorful little aprons under her arm, Nelly Don—her own first saleswoman—ventured forth to interview the buyer in a large Kansas City department store. To her this step was a venture into a hitherto unknown, formidable field. Little did she know of the rules and regulations of salesmanship, or the habits of shrewd buyers—but she was undaunted. She had unbounded confidence in her goods—the first requisite of success. She knew, or thought she knew, what women wanted. She knew they liked her aprons—she thought the aprons would speak for themselves —*and they did.*

More pages from "A Modern Business Romance." Top left is a photograph from around 1928 with Paul Donnelly and Nell in the middle between two unknown travelers. It appears they are on vacation in the Rockies. The car in this photograph is the same Lincoln that Nell was kidnapped in.

The Apron String Kept Stretching

FROM city to city—from hamlet to hamlet—women had heard—buyers had heard about these little aprons—these bright little Nelly Dons that were everywhere peeping forth in the house dress departments like bright little crocuses among the usually drab surroundings. Almost as quick as they appeared they were sold and went out into the homes of the community to make the mother, the woman in the home, the picture she should be—the picture this young bride wanted to be herself, felt every woman should be in her own home.

Then The Chic Little Nelly Dons Began to "Come Out of the Kitchen"

WHEN she made those first pretty pink aprons to wear in her own kitchen, little did Nelly Don realize what the future held for her. Imbued in the beginning only with the thought that she could fill a need ... could render a service to women such as she had sought and could not find ... she found an untouched field awaiting her creative hand.

In the confidence and inspiration of women ... in endeavoring to keep

Now Nelly Dons Are Worn From Sun to Sun

A Nelly Don wardrobe today may include not only an assortment of the original morning apron frocks, but there are soft little afternoon dresses, smart tailored sport frocks, there are styles for school, for business, for vacation wear, and for every informal occasion. Women have learned that in Nelly Dons they can have several frocks for the price they so often paid for one no more attractive, no more perfectly finished dress.

Today Nelly Don customers include not

Origin of the Name

Donnelly

Don Nelly

Nelly Don

Nelly Don is an inversion of the name Donnelly. It worked because it was a little bit of Nell and a little bit of Paul.

Nell (c. 1926).

This print is one in a series depicting Nelly Don fashions in the 1920s, 1930s and 1940s. The two images at far right are promotional items. Nell innately understood the power and necessity of relentless marketing.

Chapter Three

From County Cork, Ireland, to Jackson County, Missouri

Nell was first generation American Irish. Her father, John Quinlan emigrated from County Cork, Ireland, to America at some point before the Civil War. He was a teenager when he made the long voyage and is said to have chosen to land in New Orleans rather than New York or Boston because of the prejudice against the Irish in those cities.

John Quinlan worked as a livery servant for a wealthy man in the Garden District of New Orleans. Apparently his employer took a liking to John because he opened up his library to the young man and let him read to his heart's content. John is said to have been a "Hedge School" student while in Ireland, taught secretly by Catholic priests due to British proscription laws against Irish education. John Quinlan was literate when he left Ireland which served him well in America.

According to Nell, her father considered America "the beacon light of the world" and as such was opposed to splitting the country up and thus sided with the Union politically. With the approbation of his employer, he left New Orleans and headed north to Illinois where he enlisted in the Union Army in 1862, but just a few months later he was discharged for an unknown disability. In Illinois, he met his wife Catherine Fitzgibbons, daughter of Irish immigrants, and together they had 13 children.

The Quinlan family eventually settled near the town of Parsons, in southeastern Kansas, where John was a farmer and then worked for the Katy Railroad. Nell was the 12th child in the family and the youngest of five daughters. She learned to sew from her mother and her oldest sister Mary. She not only repaired and remade the dresses handed down

Continued on Page 28

John Quinlan 　　　　　Catherine Fitzgibbons Quinlan

Top, Nell's parents in 19th century photographs. John Quinlan emigrated from County Cork, Ireland, to America where he met his wife Catherine Fitzgibbons, the daughter of parents who had emigrated from Ireland.

Above is a photo of the inside of a 19th century cottage in Ireland, souvenirs from a trip Nell took with the author's grandmother Kate McCormick Baty in the early 1930s.

At left is a photo of Nell (c. 1894). She used to sew dresses for her playdolls.

From County Cork, Ireland, to Jackson County, Missouri

Nell is second from left and the other child is Kate McCormick Baty, who is the daughter of Mary Quinlan McCormick, Nell's oldest sister seated to the far right. Nell's other sisters are Katie (far left) and Hannah (standing center).

Photo of Nell's brothers Ed, John and Joe Quinlan (c. 1896).

Photograph of Parsons, Kansas, in the 1890s, when Nell grew up there.

Another photo of Nell and Kate McCormick Baty. Nell was just three years older than her niece and they grew up like sisters. They were lifelong friends and Kate would later be Nell's Matron of Honor when she married Sen. James A. Reed.

Nell's brother Harry has his arm around baby Nell. Harry's son, Jack Quinlan, would one day be President of Nelly Don.

Continued from Page 26

from her older sisters, but she also sewed original dresses for the dolls she so loved. Perhaps it is her experimentation with doll fashions that gave Nell the confidence to make dresses later on.

Nell once remarked that to understand growing up in Parsons at the end of the 19th century, all one had to do was see the musical "Oklahoma," because they "got the atmosphere exactly right." The Quinlan family was not dirt poor, but it certainly was not wealthy and as soon as each child was able, he or she was expected to make their own way in the world.

Nell graduated from Parsons High School and then attended Parsons Business College where she learned stenography. At age 16 she moved on her own to a boardinghouse in Kansas City where she met 23 year-old Paul Donnelly from St. Louis, who also was a stenographer. Nell and Paul were married in 1906 when Nell was 17 years-old.

Shortly after their nuptials, Nell confided to Paul that she wanted to continue her education. Paul Donnelly encouraged her and even put up the $900 to enroll Nell at Lindenwood College in St. Charles, Missouri, near St. Louis. Nell graduated from Lindenwood in 1909 and she and Paul resettled in Kansas City where Nell became a housewife, but not for long.

Postcard photograph of Kansas City (c. 1905), around the time when Nell moved to KC.

Nell was just 16 years old when she moved to Kansas City and met Paul Donnelly. The photograph above is the earliest known photo of Nell as a young woman.

At far right is Nell in her wedding dress as a 17 year-old bride in 1906.

From County Cork, Ireland, to Jackson County, Missouri

SENIOR TENNIS CLUB.

Nell Quinlan Donnelly, President.
Virginia Louise Betts, Vice-President.

Ethel Maurine Allen.   Helen Vaughn Babcock.
Carrie E. Collins.   Alice N. Ripley.
            Marie Krebs.

LINDENWOOD HALL   HALLS OF RESIDENCE   JUBILEE HALL

Nell was a married student at Lindenwood College in St. Charles, MO, near St. Louis. She was President of the Tennis Club (upper left), Secretary of the Phi Delta Sigma sorority (center) and a member of the "Boys Chorus" (lower left). Nell's 1909 yearbook photo is on the bottom right.

Chapter Four

We're In The Money!

By the time Paul Donnelly returned from World War I in 1919 (it is unknown whether he ever saw combat), Nell's enterprise had grown to 18 employees, had $250,000 in sales and was completely debt free.

At that point they formed the Donnelly Garment Company with Paul as President overseeing sales and finances and Nell taking the lesser title of Secretary/Treasurer, designing all the dresses and supervising production. It was a real "Modern Business Romance" and they promoted it that way.

By 1923, seven years after that first big order from Peck's, the Donnelly Garment Company had 250 employees and Nelly Don dresses were sold in most major department stores around the country.

By 1929, the Donnelly Garment Company employed 1,000 people and was making 5,000 dresses a day. Nelly Dons were sold nationwide and in Canada and Europe. Nell and Paul were making so many dresses of their exclusive designs that Nell ordered patterns and color schemes directly from fabric mills, eliminating brokers and further reducing costs. Nell traveled to Paris and Vienna to study new styles and get fresh ideas.

In 1931, the Donnelly Garment Company manufactured 1.5 million dresses and had $3.5 million in sales (which means the average price of a dress was $2.33). Paul and Nell were millionaires and enjoyed a life of absolute wealth, able to afford virtually anything they wanted even in the midst of the Great Depression.

It is written that Paul Donnelly had always wanted to own his own company, but that he never imagined it would be dress manufacturing. While Paul obviously had a keen instinct for business, his passion for dressmaking could never match Nell's. Further, Nell became "Nelly Don," an

The "Roaring Twenties" were especially good to Nell and Paul. The Donnelly Garment Company grew every year making Paul and Nell quite wealthy.

Nelly Don dresses were in such high demand that department stores wanting to sell them had to do so exclusively, carrying no other brands of dresses. Hundreds of stores around the country established Nelly Don dress shops within their stores. The name Nelly Don meant quality and affordability and the Nelly Don shops became destination points for millions of American women.

At left is a photograph of Nell exuding great confidence (c. 1926).

We're In The Money!

Studio photos of Nell (c. 1925).

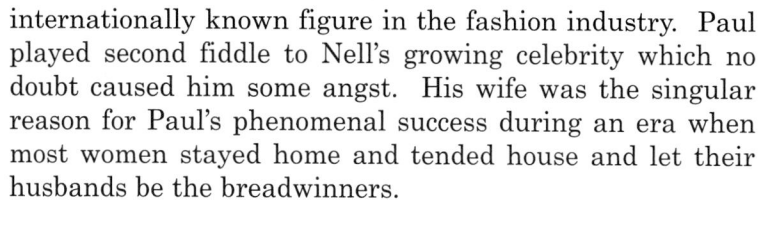

internationally known figure in the fashion industry. Paul played second fiddle to Nell's growing celebrity which no doubt caused him some angst. His wife was the singular reason for Paul's phenomenal success during an era when most women stayed home and tended house and let their husbands be the breadwinners.

1923 panorama photo of the Donnelly Garment Company on top of the Coca Cola Building in Kansas City. Nell is third from the left in the front row standing next to Paul. At this time, the company was just 7 years old.

NELLY DON: A Stitch In Time

Nell and Paul during the 1920s, enjoying success and wealth. The photo below is a studio portrait of them, while the photo at left is a personal family photo (c. 1924). At far left, Nell models a Nelly Don ensemble complete with hat. Nell considered herself to be a mid-size woman, not petite, but not real big either.

We're In The Money!   33

The top photo shows Paul (far left) with Nell next to him and two unknown traveling companions (c. 1928).

At right is Nell modeling around 1925. Nell always wore her own fashions at work and those women who were office workers were also expected to wear Nelly Dons.

At far right are Nell and Paul (c. 1928).

NELLY DON: A Stitch In Time

More Nelly Don shops. At far top left is the foyer to Nell's office at the factory. Bottom right is Paul Donnelly (left), an unknown traveling companion (center) and Nell (c. 1928).

Mabley & Carew

★

The new Nelly Dons are here!

PRICED FROM 1.95 TO 10.95

Kansas City was a major player in the national garment industries, at its peak boasting no fewer than 25 garment manufacturers, with Nelly Don, of course, the largest of them all. The "Market News" at left was a fashion trade magazine published in Kansas City.

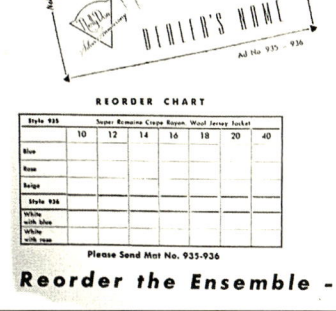

Chapter Five

The Older the Fiddler, The Sweeter the Tune!

(Irish Proverb)

Nell was pretty sweet on Jim Reed when Reed was in his mid-to-late 60s in the late 1920s. Nell's marriage to Paul Donnelly was on the wane due to Paul's drinking and philandering and the dashing retired U.S. Senator was alluring to Nell.

James Alexander Reed stood about six feet, two inches tall and was a slender man with a full head of hair. Even if one disagreed with Reed's views, nobody could deny that he was a commanding presence in the Senate.

At age 26, while an attorney in Cedar Rapids, Iowa, Jim had an affair with a married woman named Lura Olmstead who, at age 43, was 17 years older than Jim. The scandal resulted in Lura's husband divorcing her and a hasty marriage between Jim and Lura. The couple then moved to Kansas City in 1887 for Jim to practice law.

Reed quickly made a name for himself through his aggressive style and florid oratory. He attracted the attention of Jim Pendergast, powerful alderman for the west bottoms of Kansas City who was laying the foundation for what would become one of the most powerful and enduring political machines in the country. With Pendergast's backing, Reed was elected Jackson County prosecutor in 1898 and Mayor in 1900.

As mayor, Reed appointed Pendergast's younger brother, Tom, Superintendant of Streets. That act would have profound ramifications for the rest of the country in the years to come. As superintendant, Tom learned about paving and concrete and would go on to form the Ready-Mix Concrete Company. Under that guise, Tom expanded control of the Pendergast machine begun by his brother and it was under this corrupt, political structure that Harry Truman rose to

James Alexander Reed
U.S. Senator, Missouri
Democrat (1911-1929)

prominence. Reed and Tom Pendergast maintained a professional relationship the rest of their careers, exchanging correspondence and political favors for one another.

In 1911, Reed was elected to the United States Senate where he became known as "the fighting senator from Missouri". As senator, Reed parted with his fellow Democrats in opposing America joining the League of Nations. Reed also vehemently opposed prohibition and its attendant hypocrisy. On numerous occasions, he threatened to expose those Congressman who "vote dry and drink wet." Reed also opposed the women's suffrage movement contending that women would vote the same as their husbands and it would merely duplicate the vote.

Back home in Missouri, resentment and opposition to Reed's provocative style was polarizing. Reed was refused credentials at the 1920 Democratic Presidential Convention in San Francisco, and a "Rid us of Reed" movement was formed by Missouri women offended by his strident views.

But Reed was not without his supporters. William Randolph Hearst, the newspaper magnate liked Reed's pugilistic politics and supported Reed's later presidential aspirations. After being locked out of the Democratic convention in 1920, Reed returned home to Kansas City where a reported 8,000 people turned out at the train station to show their support.

So Reed was re-elected to the Senate for a third term in 1922. He made a national name for himself by attacking election corruption and fraud. He exposed the questionable circumstances under which two Senators-elect won their elections, thus preventing either man from ever serving in the Senate.

Reed tested the presidential waters in 1924, but there was still too much resentment of him within party ranks. But by 1928, Reed had national recognition, and formally declared his candidacy for president.

Coincidentally, during this period Reed's home in Kansas City sat adjacent to Paul and Nell Donnelly's home. Nell and Reed both kept large dogs and shared a dog run between their houses.

In late February 1928, Nell Donnelly strolled in unan-

Jim Reed was born November 9, 1861 in Cedar Rapids, Iowa. Top left is Jim about five years of age already looking like he's ready to take on all comers (c. 1866).

Top right, is the earliest known photo of Reed as a young attorney probably in Cedar Rapids, Iowa (c. 1887).

Above is Jim Reed as a young attorney in Kansas City (c. 1894).

Right is Jim Reed's official mayoral portrait when he served as Kansas City Mayor from 1900 to 1904.

```
                T. J. PENDERGAST
                 KANSAS CITY, MO.




Hon. James A. Reed
Telephone Bldg
City

My Dear Mr. Reed,
              I wish to introduce to you Mrs.
Ruth J. Rubel, who has a proposition I feel sure
will be of interested to you, and I take this opp-
ortunity of recommending her ability. She is well
qualified in her line of business and capable of
handling all of its phases and has had a very success-
ful experience. She has as her clientele the repres-
entative business and professional men of Kansas City,
many of whom are our friends and associates.

              I am sure you will be pleased with
any business you do with Mrs. Rubel. Thanking you for
your courtesies to her and the cooperation you may give
her, I am

                        Faithfully yours,
                        T. J. Pendergast
```

JAMES PENDERGAST,
Alderman Lower House, 1st Ward

THOMAS PENDERGAST,
Superintendent of Streets.

Top left is typical correspondence from Tom Pendergast to Reed. They exchanged numerous political favors for one another over the course of more than 30 years.

Top center is Alderman Jim Pendergast, older brother of Tom and the originator of what became the most powerful political machine in Kansas City.

Top right is a young Tom Pendergast from the official 1901 Kansas City Blue Book, a publication of government officials. Reed appointed Pendergast as Superintendent of Streets, an act that had far reaching consequences.

Lower left is a young Lura Olmstead Reed. Lura was married and 17 years older than Reed when she had an affair with him in Cedar Rapids, Iowa. Lura's husband divorced her and she quickly married Reed and moved with him to KC.

Right, Harry S. Truman, rose politically under the machine controlled by Tom Pendergast. Truman was not a big fan of Jim Reed.

nounced to Reed's presidential campaign headquarters in Washington D.C. A staffer was stunned as Nell presented a check contributing $1,000. Only William Randolph Hearst personally contributed more to Reed's presidential campaign.

But Reed could not compete with the campaign organization of New York Governor Al Smith and Reed came in third place in balloting at the 1928 Democratic Convention.

As a result, the 66 year-old Reed opted to not seek a fourth term as Senator, but instead return to private law practice in Kansas City.

SENATOR REED CALLS LEAGUE OF NATIONS A COLOSSAL FRAUD

"SAY RATIFICATION!"

SENATOR REED FLAYS WORLD LEAGUE AS MENACE TO AMERICA'S FREEDOM

He Says That England Has Great Advantage Thru Covenant.

REED ATTACKS WORLD LEAGUE AS MENACE TO U.S. FREEDOM

In Auditorium Speech He Says England Gets Great Advantage.

Attacking the covenant of the League of Nations as an instrument which, if adopted, would mean "hauling down the Stars and Stripes and raising in its place the dirty rag of internationalism," Senator James A. Reed of Missouri Saturday night delivered a two-and-a-half-hour talk to an audience of 8,000 persons at the Auditorium.

Senator Reed confined himself solely to the league covenant throut his argument. He took issue with President Wilson's statement that Great Britain's six votes will have only the effect of one vote, and declared that the British colonies represented in the proposed international assembly...

UNITED STATES SENATOR JAMES A. REED SNAPPED ON HIS ARRIVAL AT THE UNION STATION WITH SOME OF THE PROMINENT DENVERITES WHO MET HIM.

Left to right: State Auditor Arthur M. Stong, A. M. Stevenson, John T. Bottom, John Sandberg, Gen. Emmett Newton, who is accompanying Senator Reed; S. R. Fitzgerald, S. D. Nicholson, Congressman William N. Vaile, Mrs. John T. Bottom, W. H. Dickson, Mrs. James A. Reed, Senator Reed, Benjamin C. Hilliard and L. J. Stark. At the bottom is a close-up view of Senator Reed.

"I am compelled, in fact, to challenge every statement that the president has made about the assembly.

"It was brought out recently in the examination before the military committee of the United States senate that it is proposed to form a great corporation in this country for the purpose of organizing trade with Europe. The house of Morgan is to be at the neck of a great stream of supplies, and another corporation is to be formed to allocate these supplies to Europe...

States is to be drawn upon to help... supplies and money are to be secured by the bonds of European governments..."

SEES CHAOS IN A LEAGUE

THIS COUNTRY WOULD BE LIKE RUSSIA, SAYS REED.

Missouri Senator Shows How Covenant Would Hand Over Reins of Government to Labor Mass—Refers to Ardmore Incident.

"International Bolshevism is creeping into the United States in the guise of the League of Nations, and will wreak the same chaos in this country that it has in Russia..."

Reed broke ranks with fellow Democrats in opposing the League of Nations. Woodrow Wilson was embittered toward Reed for his opposition. Reed followed Wilson around the country denouncing what Reed perceived as a threat to America's national security interests.

Reed Is Welcomed Home Like a Conquering Hero

[Kansas City Journal, Tuesday, July 6, 1920]

OPPOSITION TO WOMEN HELD AS REED'S MISTAKE

Delegate Explains Why Missouri Delegate Lost His Convention Seat

Thumbs Down for Senator Reed, Is Verdict of Women

By Frances Jolliffe.

This drama is called "Retribution" or "Woman Triumphant." The cast includes:

THE MAN—Senator James A. Reed of Missouri, once leader of his party in Missouri, now a political nobody in San Francisco.

THE WOMAN—Personifying the womanhood of Missouri—Mrs. W. W. Martin, delegate from the Fourteenth Missouri District, officer of State Board of Equal Suffrage Association, press chairman of Missouri Federation of Women's Clubs, Missouri committee, National League of Women Voters.

Reed vehemently opposed prohibition and its attendant hypocrisy. Above left is a book of speeches by Reed attacking Prohibition.

Reed unwisely opposed the Women's Suffrage Movement, causing Missouri women to form a "Rid Us of Reed" coalition that was instrumental in locking Reed out from the Democratic National Convention in 1920.

Despite Reed's polarizing politics, many Missourians liked Reed's willingness to fight on principal notwithstanding the political consequences. When Reed returned to Kansas City after being locked out of the Democratic National Convention in 1920, some eight thousand persons were at Union Station to show support. Reed won re-election in 1922 and served a third term in the U.S. Senate.

the Older the Fiddler, The Sweeter the Tune!

A "Reed for President" button from the 1928 campaign.

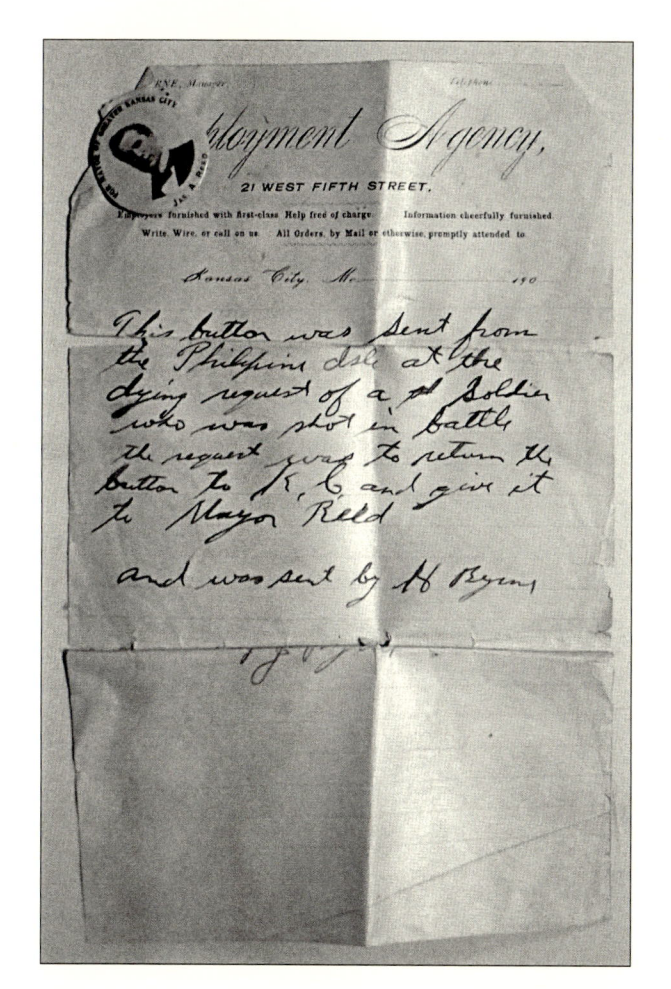

Left is a letter enclosing a button of Reed from a dying American soldier who carried it with him into battle in the Phillipines and requested that it be returned to "Mayor Reed."

Reed was a favorite subject of political cartoonists because he was always arguing and fighting with Republicans and Democrats alike.

Reed gained national attention for attacking election fraud in the 1920s. He was a legitimate presidential candidate in 1928 but lost the nomination to Al Smith, Governor of New York, whose Tammany Hall organization Reed could not match.

Reed retired from the Senate in 1929 and returned to Kansas City to practice law. He represented Henry Ford in a libel lawsuit and was considered one of the top trial lawyers in the country.

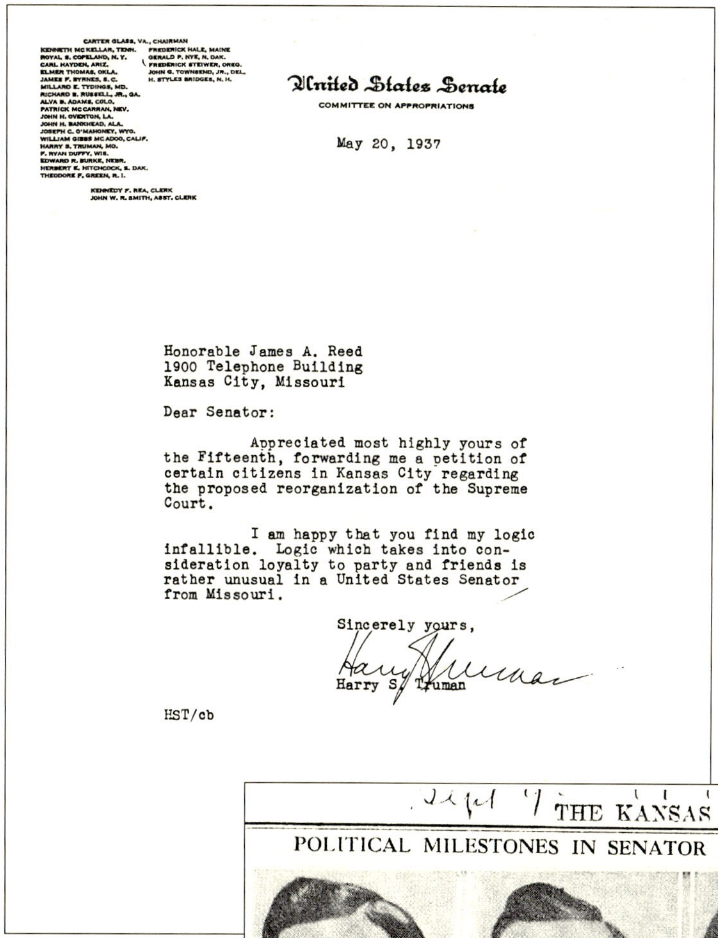

the Older the Fiddler, The Sweeter the Tune!

43

United States Senate
COMMITTEE ON APPROPRIATIONS

May 20, 1937

Honorable James A. Reed
1900 Telephone Building
Kansas City, Missouri

Dear Senator:

Appreciated most highly yours of the Fifteenth, forwarding me a petition of certain citizens in Kansas City regarding the proposed reorganization of the Supreme Court.

I am happy that you find my logic infallible. Logic which takes into consideration loyalty to party and friends is rather unusual in a United States Senator from Missouri.

Sincerely yours,

Harry S. Truman

HST/cb

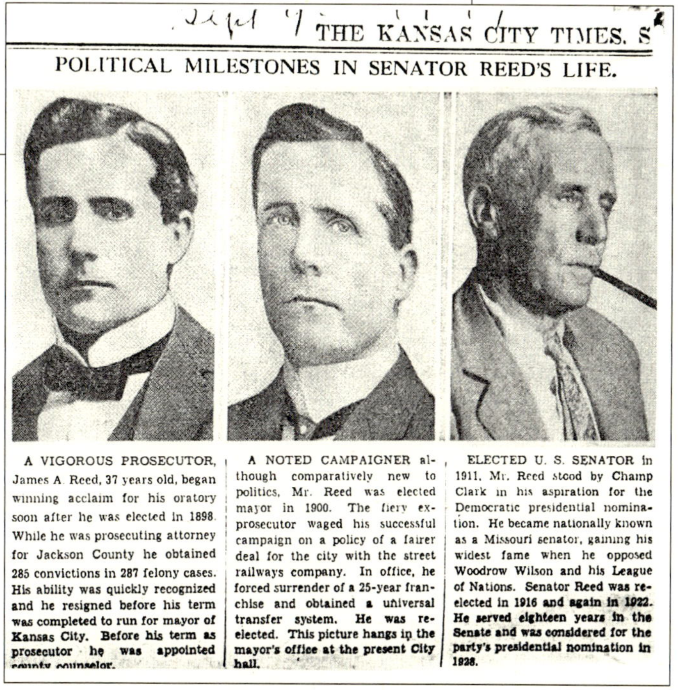

Reed never authored any major legislation of his own, but his support of bills was critical because of the vociferous manner in which he attacked bills he did not like.

Top Right is a letter from Harry S. Truman to Reed after Reed had been retired from the Senate eight years. The letter takes a not too subtle jab at Reed for not being loyal to "party and friends." Reed was a vocal opponent of FDR's New Deal Politics.

Right is a summation of Reed's career by the Kansas City Times newspaper.

THE KANSAS CITY TIMES.
POLITICAL MILESTONES IN SENATOR REED'S LIFE.

A VIGOROUS PROSECUTOR, James A. Reed, 37 years old, began winning acclaim for his oratory soon after he was elected in 1898. While he was prosecuting attorney for Jackson County he obtained 285 convictions in 287 felony cases. His ability was quickly recognized and he resigned before his term was completed to run for mayor of Kansas City. Before his term as prosecutor he was appointed county counselor.

A NOTED CAMPAIGNER although comparatively new to politics, Mr. Reed was elected mayor in 1900. The fiery ex-prosecutor waged his successful campaign on a policy of a fairer deal for the city with the street railways company. In office, he forced surrender of a 25-year franchise and obtained a universal transfer system. He was re-elected. This picture hangs in the mayor's office at the present City hall.

ELECTED U. S. SENATOR in 1911, Mr. Reed stood by Champ Clark in his aspiration for the Democratic presidential nomination. He became nationally known as a Missouri senator, gaining his widest fame when he opposed Woodrow Wilson and his League of Nations. Senator Reed was re-elected in 1916 and again in 1922. He served eighteen years in the Senate and was considered for the party's presidential nomination in 1928.

Jim Reed Retires From Senate, Assured of Niche in Hall of Fame, as True Example of Man Who Would 'Rather Be Right Than President'

Veteran Protected Nation, at Own Expense, in Fight for Higher Ideals.

By HORACE H. HERR

Of The Journal-Post Washington Bureau.

WASHINGTON, Feb. 23.—Those who have tears to shed, if one may bootleg a Mark Anthony phrase, prepare to reserve them for a more lachrymose occasion. We are not here to bury Caesar and surely not to praise him.

We are here to observe that Sen. James A. Reed of Missouri reverts to the status quo ante on March 4; to felicitate him on his return to private life with his pristine glory unsullied and his Americanism not yet cut to the ½ of 1 per cent standard of these hectic days.

To indicate the broad, nonpartisan attitude in which this chore is approached, one may digress to congratulate Herbert Hoover on the prospect that there will remain in the chamber of stentorian efforts no one likely to cramp the presidential style.

It would be sheer niggardliness to refrain from including in this congratulatory impulse, the United States senate. The retirement of the Missouri Democrat will make for peace and harmony. It will make the Republican majority invincible and the Democratic minority invisible.

Admitting he was out of place in a medley of mediocrity and granting he often took mean advantage of its senility, yet it may be submitted that Senator Reed of Missouri served a...

SENATOR REED AND THE STATE COMMITTEE

Retirement from the Senate did little to slow Reed down. He practiced law with vigor and tried both civil and criminal cases.

In recognition of his unswerving devotion to the principles of George Washington, eighty-six Senators requested Reed to read Washington's Farewell address upon Reed's retirement from the Senate (1929).

'Fighting Jim' Reed Shows Milder Side With Return to Home and Canine Pal

Eye Loses Steely Glint as He Gives Surroundings Approval.

By H. G. THOMPSON.

There was a quietness yesterday at the Reed home, 5236 Cherry street, that seemed to portray something of the life that former Senator Reed will lead from now on. He had ridden from the Union station in a car belonging to Cyril Lechtman. Mrs. Reed had followed in the Reed car, driven by their chauffeur. A motorcycle police escort had accompanied them to their home.

As he stepped from the car, Reed paused for a moment and glanced about, as if to accustom himself to the home where he will pass the remainder of his years with Mrs. Reed and his dog "Jeff."

Then a smile spread over his face and he turned and shook hands with each member of the police escort and thanked them for their services.

The car in which Mrs. Reed was riding drew up behind her husband's car, but she did not alight until photographers had taken several pictures. Reed then turned and assisted her from the car.

More Gentle Light in Eyes.

As he walked slowly up the walk to the front door of his home he again glanced about the yard and looked at the house. The fighting light that has shown in his eyes so many years receded and a gentleness few persons have seen him show bespoke the pleasure he seemed to feel as he realized that at last he could rest in his home far away from the political battlefield on which he has stood for thirty years.

Mrs. Reed accompanied by Mrs. J. W. McMurray and Mrs. Ed S. Vilmoore went up to the front door and rang the bell. There was no response, and Mrs. Reed said:

"Perhaps she did not hear," and rang the bell again.

This time there was a movement inside and the door was opened by the maid.

"Oh, there you are," the maid said.

"Oh, my dear Mrs. Reed, I am so glad to see you."

Puts Arm Around Maid.

Mrs. Reed grasped her hand and then put an arm around her shoulder and said:

"Oh, how good it seems to be home at last."

There was another movement inside the house and a smile spread over Reed's face as "Jeff," the police dog, burst through the doorway

the Older the Fiddler, The Sweeter the Tune!   45

Top right is a Christmas card to Reed from Gutzon Borglum, the sculptor of Mt. Rushmore. Bottom right is a bust of Reed by Borglum.

The photo of Reed (top left) shows him around 1920 when he was locked out of the Democratic National Convention. Upon Reed's retirement from the Senate, famed Baltimore Sun columnist H.L. Mencken published in the American Mercury a glowing tribute to Reed and the principles for which he fought.

H. L. Mencken

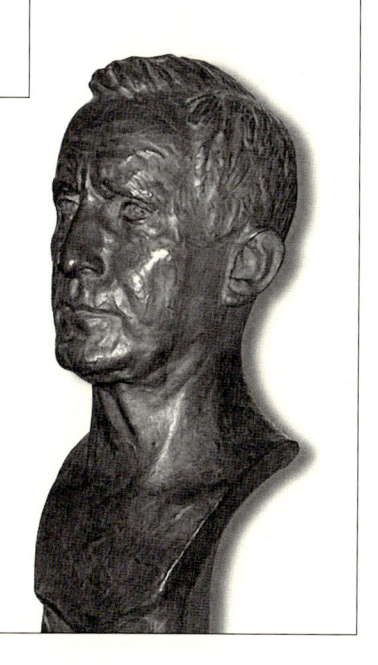

Reed's inveterate cigar smoking helped cartoonists parody the "Fighting Senator from Missouri."

Chapter Six

Handy Dandy to the Rescue

When the stock market crashed in 1929, Nell worried about her workers, most of whom were women. She knew that many husbands and fathers would be losing their jobs and the money her employees earned might be the only household income. Up until this time, the Donnelly Garment Company employed the majority of its workers on a seasonal basis for the summer and winter lines of fashion.

But around 1925, Nell patented the Handy Dandy Apron. The Handy-Dandy protected a woman's clothing in the kitchen and was made to hold utensils, oven mitts and the like. Nell designed it to make women attractive while preparing meals. But its genius was in manufacturing because a seamstress never had to remove the garment from the machine to sew the seams, thus cutting down on production time and making them affordable. Nelly Don made millions of these simple aprons and Nell used the Handy Dandy to keep the factory open year-round.

Nelly Don sold millions of Handy Dandy aprons, which helped keep the factory open year round, and gave employment to many people at the start of the Depression. Nell had to prosecute her patent of the Handy Dandy in an infringement suit in 1928 in St. Louis. Nell used much of the cash generated by Handy Dandy sales to buy out Paul Donnelly's interest in the company.

Nell also understood that women did not want to always wear dresses and so she also designed slacks and overall ensembles for women to wear at leisure.

Above right is perhaps the most famous photograph of Nell as a young woman (c. 1926).

Handy Dandy to the Rescue

Some photos of Nell relaxing at her home from where she was kidnapped (c. 1930). Reed had arranged for Nell and Paul Donnelly to lease the home directly behind his house where he and Lura lived. A dog run adjoined the two properties. It is during this period that Nell and Reed coalesced even though both were married to other people.

Chapter Seven

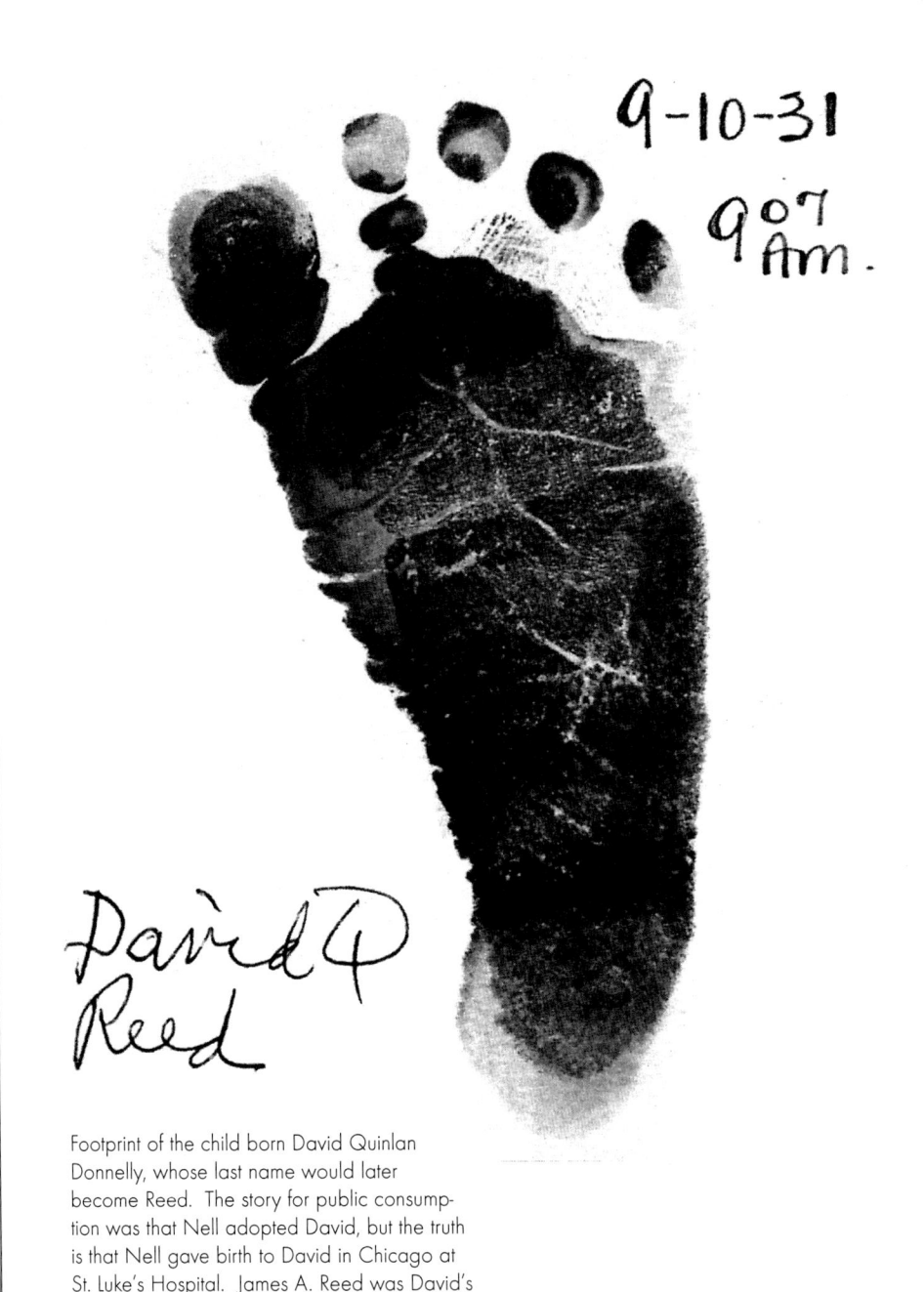

David Quinlan Donnelly Reed

By 1930, Nell was married to Paul Donnelly in name only. Paul was a philandering dipsomaniac and after he hurled an ashtray at Nell over the dinner table one night, Nell knew then her marriage was over.

In hindsight, it is clear that Paul was manic depressive. He threatened Nell on numerous occasions that if Nell became pregnant, he would kill himself.

Being the 12th of 13 children, Nell had great extended family and was benevolent with her wealth. But Nell wanted her own family, her own child, and in the summer of 1931 at age 42, Nell traveled to Europe with her trusted niece Kate McCormick Baty, ostensibly to adopt a child.

The truth, as told by those close to her, is that Nell was pregnant and on September 10, 1931, at St. Luke's Hospital in Chicago, Nell gave birth to a healthy boy she named David Quinlan Donnelly and returned to Kansas City with her adopted child.

Today Reed family members accede with pride that James A. Reed was the natural and biological father of David Q. Reed. Around 1930, Reed arranged for Paul and Nell to lease a mansion directly behind Reed's home. It is presumed that when Nell became pregnant that both she and Reed approached Paul Donnelly and impressed upon him that if he failed to remain discreet his entire fortune could be lost. Scandal could devastate the business.

Lest there be any doubt as to Reed's attachment to Nell, an event three months after David's birth would give stage to Reed's intense affection for the mother of his only child.

Footprint of the child born David Quinlan Donnelly, whose last name would later become Reed. The story for public consumption was that Nell adopted David, but the truth is that Nell gave birth to David in Chicago at St. Luke's Hospital. James A. Reed was David's father.

David Quinlan Donnelly Reed

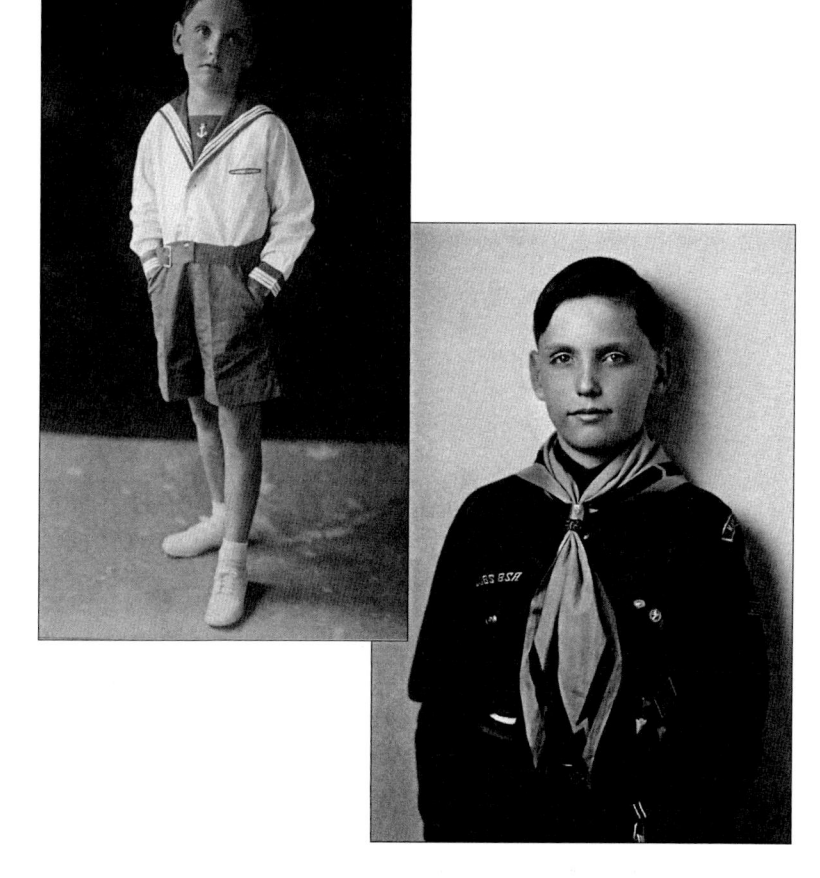

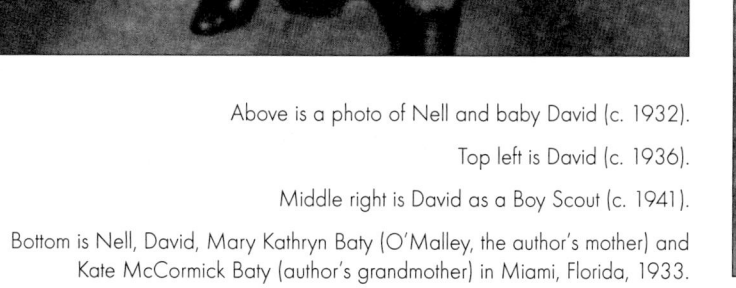

Above is a photo of Nell and baby David (c. 1932).

Top left is David (c. 1936).

Middle right is David as a Boy Scout (c. 1941).

Bottom is Nell, David, Mary Kathryn Baty (O'Malley, the author's mother) and Kate McCormick Baty (author's grandmother) in Miami, Florida, 1933.

Chapter Eight

The Kidnapping

On the evening of December 16, 1931, Nell left her office at the factory in downtown Kansas City riding in a 1928 Lincoln convertible sedan driven by her chauffeur, 28 year-old George Blair.

Shortly after 6 p.m., the Lincoln approached the Donnelly home driveway entrance that was blocked by another car. George Blair sounded his car horn and rolled down the window to ask the men hovering over the engine to move the car. Suddenly three men rushed the car and overpowered Nell and George and transported them out to a remote farmhouse and forced Nell to write ransom notes indicating that if $75,000 was not paid, they were going to blind Nell and kill George Blair.

Reed was in trial in Jefferson City, Missouri, about 150 miles from KC. Upon hearing the news of Nell's kidnapping, he rushed from the courtroom thus drawing the attention of some reporters on hand who figured out what was going on and contacted their editors in Kansas City to inform them of Nell's abduction.

When Reed got to the Donnelly home, he issued a bold statement taking blame for publication of the abduction and then threatened the kidnappers that if they harmed one hair on Nell's head he would spend the rest of his life tracking them down and ensuring they received the death penalty.

Reed then got hold of Johnny Lazia, a political gangster in Kansas City, who delivered votes to Tom Pendergast's candidates in exchange for police protection for Lazia's gambling and vice operations.

When told of Nell's abduction, Lazia informed Reed that it would make no sense for the KC Mob to kidnap a prominent member of the business community and attract attention to

Nell and George's abduction on December 16, 1931, made headlines all over the country.

This photograph shows contents retrieved from Nell's car abandoned behind the Plaza Theater in Kansas City's Country Club District. In addition to a hat, gloves and umbrella, there were two checkbooks, one of which had bloodstains on it and a piece of rope with red flecks of paint on it which, according to a published account, was a major clue.

This photo of Nell is from the August 1943 True Detective Magazine detailing how gangsters solved the kidnapping.

The Kidnapping

it. Reed threatened Lazia that if Lazia did not find Nell within 24 hours Reed would buy a half-hour of national radio time and expose Lazia and his corrupt operations and influence in Kansas City.

Lazia is said to have sent 25 carloads of hoodlums looking for Nell. Through some amazing detective work they found where Nell was and rescued her from her abductors. She and George had been in captivity for 34 hours. But Lazia would not reveal the identity of the kidnappers; the Police were on their own. Eventually the ringleader of the failed crime was tracked to South Africa and extradited to Kansas City. Two of the kidnappers received life sentences and one was sentenced to 35 years in prison.

Top right, The Kansas City Star obtained the original ransom note dictated by the gang leader and written by Nell under flashlight.

The middle photograph is attorney James Taylor, counsel for the Donnelly Garment Company who received a phone message about where the Donnelly car could be found. He thought the caller had him confused with another James Taylor and went to bed.

Below is the 1928 Ford Lincoln driven by Nell's chauffeur George Blair at the time of the kidnapping.

Bottom right is Nell and Paul Donnelly's home in Kansas City that is now a toy & miniature museum.

MRS. NELL DONNELLY'S LETTER NOTIFYING HER HUSBAND OF THE KIDNAPING AND THE TERMS OF RANSOM.

Dear Paul
These men say they want 75000 Use your own judgment they kidnapped me & chauffeur Wed night & If you do not pay as directed 75000 in cash 25.000 in $50 bills 25 000 in 20's 25 000 in 10's. If he or any does not do as directed we shall take him same as taken you if reported to police or any authorities we shall blind you and kill nigger. You should take your car 291035 tomorrow at 10 o'clock and stand it in front of Mercer Hotel for 15 minutes that is showing that you are ready to pay. If not stand it at same place at 9 30 am Fri. morning If not ready then it will cost you 25 000 more then showing when you are ready to stand there at that said point any one of those times for 15 minutes, other go home and you will receive further instructions. Remember if this is reported to police you will not see me again.

RANSOM OF $75,000 BEING DEMANDED FOR MRS. NELL DONNELLY

Held by Kidnapers

Mrs. Nell Q. Donnelly of the Donnelly Garment company, who was kidnaped last night and is being held for $75,000 ransom.

Million Dollar Idea Born of Need to Remake Sister's Clothes for Self

Mrs. Nell Donnelly Youngest of Family of Twelve Children, Born on Little Farm Near Parsons, Kas.

A million dollar idea, born of the necessity of "making over" her older sisters' clothes for herself, tied the apron strings of Mrs. Nell Donnelly on 1,000,000 others of her sex in all corners of the world and made her one of the outstanding business women of the United States.

The idea was house dresses, the business she developed is the Donnelly Garment company, and the story of the manner in which she brought it to its present high pinnacle is one of the business romances of Kansas City.

Mrs. Donnelly was born on a little farm near Parsons, Kas., the youngest of the twelve Quinlan children. There were other girls in the family and the problem of properly clothing them was one which caused their parents considerable concern. So, naturally, necessity demanded that Nell, the youngest, "make over" the dresses the older sisters had outgrown and claim them for her own.

Early Aptitude With Needle.

Her aptitude with the needle was marked from the first, but none ever dreamed it would bring her wealth or an enviable position in the business life of Kansas City, where she came, after attending a convent, high school and business college in Parsons, to begin work as a stenographer.

Even she had no dreams along that line at the time. Her one ambition then was to earn and save enough money to enable her to attend college.

At the rooming house where she made her home, was another stenographer—a young man named Paul Donnelly. Nell Quinlan and Paul Donnelly had much in common; they were to confer frequently on the relative merits of the shorthand systems they had studied; must debate the superiority of the "word sign" over the "letter position," and while they did this romance bloomed and soon they were talking and writing in a language that only Cupid knows.

And so it was that when she was only 17 years old, Nell Quinlan changed her name to Donnelly, assumed her duties as helpmate for young Paul Donnelly and began the partnership which has since brought success and wealth to both of them.

Realizes College Ambition.

During the first year of their married life, Mrs. Donnelly confided to her husband that, before her marriage, she had hoped to attend college. And the young husband promptly announced that she should realize her ambition. They had been frugal, what with Mrs. Donnelly watching every penny in her purchase of groceries and making her own dresses, and some money had been saved.

Magnanimously, Paul Donnelly announced that his wife should use this money to attend college. There was considerable talk, but the husband carried his point. And Mrs. Donnelly went to school.

Following her graduation, she returned to her home in Kansas City, and for seven years she proved herself to be a model housewife. She studied the cook book, made her own clothes and found time occasionally to entertain her friends in little parties in the Donnelly home.

And always, at these parties, it was remarked that the simple little frocks she wore were among the prettiest; that she always was dressed in crisp, youthful and stylish mode.

Frocks for Gifts.

"How do you manage it?" she was asked. "Even your house dresses have chic and style." And her answer invariably was, "I make my own dresses; they are very inexpensive."

Christmas time came, and from the Donnelly home went gifts to relatives and a few friends. Among these gifts were a number of little frocks—gay, colorful dresses—which were received enthusiastically by Mrs. Donnelly's sisters and aunts and cousins.

Their appreciation was so genuine and their pleasure so real that, when one of them asked her why she did not make the frocks for sale in Kansas City stores, it planted the germ of the "million dollar" idea in her head.

She visited a number of stores next day. In each one she asked a milady:

"Haven't you anything at all in the way of a smart little dress that one can wear while doing one's housework?"

And the reply was the same. "Sorry, but we haven't. The manufacturers employ high salaried designers and they can't afford to pay them for designing inexpensive house dresses upon which there would be no profit."

"But, Mrs. Donnelly insisted, 'it's a shame to make housewives wear those ugly bungalow aprons. How can anyone like to do housework when they have to wear them?'"

The Big Idea.

Very patiently the saleladies explained:

"But, madam, it would be a waste to pay expensive designers to make such simple little garments as the dress apron."

Mrs. Donnelly boarded a street car and started home, and on that ride the big idea was born. She would make the dress aprons—would make them by the dozens, the hundreds, the—

She told Mr. Donnelly of her plan that night. He since has confessed that he was not overly enthusiastic, but, as he explains, "I always felt that Nell is smart," so he didn't offer too strenuous objections to the plan.

Then Mrs. Donnelly brought home an order for the aprons from one of the Kansas City stores, and her husband consented to install two high power machines in the Donnelly attic. Two girls were employed to sew and in a few days the "factory" was turning out two dozen aprons a day and the demand was so great for them that by noon of each day the supply was exhausted. More orders were placed and soon the little factory was taxed to capacity.

Came then the war and Mr. Donnelly entered the service, leaving his wife to carry on the business. She did, so capably that when her husband was mustered out of service he returned to Kansas City to find that the downtown offices into which he had moved the business prior to his departure soon would be too small.

Called "Nelly Don."

The business increased the name "Nelly Don" was given to the frocks and soon women in all parts of the United States were wearing them. It was then Mr. and Mrs. Donnelly decided to incorporate and the Donnelly Garment company was formed.

Today the factory is one of the largest of its kind and more than 1,000,000 "Nelly Don" dresses, worn by women from Maine to California, from Florida to North Dakota attest to the value of the idea which a desire to always appear chic in her husband's eyes gave to Nell.

"It was Mr. Donnelly who made the whole thing possible," Mrs. Donnelly says. "Of course, he gives me the credit for the idea, but where would the idea have been if the money hadn't been forthcoming?"

But today, to whomever credit should be given, the fact remains that the Donnelly Garment company is ranged as a million-dollar concern and employs approximately 1,000 workers, mostly women. It has moved from time to time as space requirements demanded, and now is located in the Corrigan building, 1828 Walnut street.

And Mrs. Donnelly, despite her intention to retire from active participation in the business when it was incorporated, still is the active head of the company, although her title on the door of the luxuriously furnished office reads, "Secretary-Treasurer."

Rght is another ransom note most likely written by kidnapper Charles Mele to Jim Reed.

Below is a picture of George Blair, Nell's chauffeur who was kidnapped wearing his chauffeur's uniform.

Below right is a bloated Paul Donnelly who was the intended kidnap victim. However, Paul was suffering one of his mysterious illnesses and had not left the home for an extended period of time. The kidnappers then settled on Nell, bad idea!

At far left is one of many newspaper articles telling the Nelly Don story at the time of the kidnapping.

MR REED
   MRS IS OK NO HARM HAS BEEN DONE TO HER SHE WILL BE HOME Sunday if you do AS TOLD if THIS LETTER GET IN PAPER OR POLICE OR Postal Authorites you WILL NEVER SEE HER AGIAN FOR BEING SO DAM SMART FOR Notifying POLICE FOR WE KNOW IF you get ANY ONE OF US IT WOULD BE DEATH SO WE CAN do THE SAME TO HER if ANY of OUR MAN ARE TAKE WHILE WE getting MONEY SHE WELL DIE WE MEAN WHAT WE SAY NO EXCUISES FROM YOU OR ANY ONE

Held With Employer

George Blair, Negro chauffeur for the Donnelly family, who was held captive by the kidnapers along with Mrs. Nell Q. Donnelly. This photograph of Blair was taken at police headquarters early Friday after Blair had given a graphic account of his experiences.

Paul Donnelly, husband of the victim. He was ill at the time of her kidnapping, but kept up a constant search by telephone in an endeavor to locate his missing wife

The Kidnapping

DEPENDS ON REED

Paul F. Donnelly Turns Ransom Affairs Over to the Former Senator.

SPEEDS HERE TO AID

As Attorney for Snyder Brothers He Was in Midst of Trial of Hahatonka Suit.

HE ISSUES A STATEMENT

Kidnapers Can Have Money if They Return Mrs. Donnelly Unharmed, Senator Asserts.

Senator James A. Reed arrived at the Paul F. Donnelly home just before 2 o'clock, having driven from Jefferson City with Kenneth Snyder, one of the plaintiffs in the suit in which Senator Reed was engaged when he received word of the kidnaping of Mrs. Donnelly.

Senator Reed brushed all questioners aside as he entered the home and with Mr. Donnelly and his law partner, James Taylor, went to an upstairs room for a conference. He said he had nothing to say for the time being.

Following the conference Senator Reed issued a statement in which he explained that it was through the manner in which he received the information of Mrs. Donnelly's abduction at Jefferson City that the facts became public.

Reed took control of managing the kidnapping affair and advocated payment of the ransom to get Nell back. In the photo below, Reed leads Paul Donnelly out of the Donnelly home during the kidnapping ordeal. Paul is holding items retrieved from Nell's car.

This is the residence of Mr. and Mrs. Paul F. Donnelly at 5235 Oak street. The kidnaping of Mrs. Donnelly is believed to have taken place in the vicinity of the home, the kidnapers forcing her Lincoln motor car, driven by a chauffeur, to the curbing.

UNDERWORLD AIDS IN KIDNAPER SEARCH

Mob Boss Johnny Lazia.

LAZIA KEEPS PLEDGE MADE ON KIDNAPING

North Side Pendergast Aide Quick to Make Good Word Given Chief.

With the wildest sort of rumors being circulated in Kansas City and with newspapers in other cities questioning whether Mrs. Nell Donnelly was released by her abductors without payment of ransom, the time has come to tell the facts.

Mrs. Donnelly WAS kidnaped.

She WAS released without the payment of ransom.

The man to whom credit is due is John Lazia, a leader in the Pendergast faction of the Democratic organization.

Kidnapers Violated Gangdom Code and Penalty Is Death, Chief Says

Underworld Expected to Run Down Members of Gang and Take Them for Ride.

The kidnapers of Mrs. Nell Donnelly and her Negro chauffeur, George Blair, have outlawed themselves so far as the underworld here is concerned and they probably will meet the gruesome fate its denizens mete out to their kind.

"They'll go for a ride," was the prediction heard Friday among those who are in constant contact with the half-world. "They'll get the works for this."

In that prediction the underworld has a backer in Chief Lewis M. Siegfried, who probably did more than any other person to bring about the return of Mrs. Donnelly and her driver unharmed.

"I think their bodies will be found out on some lonely road before we even find out who they were," the chief said. "They violated the code of gangdom and run smoothly for the rest would pull such a stunt.

"In this case at least the police system, used everywhere, of having

News of gangster Johnny Lazia's involvement in solving the kidnapping spread quickly. His men connected the piece of rope taken from Nell's car to a local gas station whose attendant remembered a man who had asked for some twine a few days earlier. That led to Victor Bonura, a local restaurant owner who drew a map to the kidnapping hideout and then quickly fled town.

The headline above quotes Kansas City's Chief of Police anticipating that the kidnappers will be taken for a ride by the Mob in KC and killed. What's striking is the soothing comfort such headlines apparently gave Kansas Citians who could be secure in knowing that professional criminals were handling the situation.

Chief Informed of Mrs. Donnelly's Release by Mysterious Phone Call

Siegfried Receives Full Directions on How to Reach Place, Then Informant Hangs Up.

The call to Chief of Police Siegfried, informing him of the liberation of Mrs. Nell Q. Donnelly and her Negro chauffeur, George Blair, reached the chief's office at 4:10 o'clock Friday morning.

The chief, after a strenuous night of telephone conversation and running down clews, was dozing in his chair when the telephone aroused him.

Chief Siegfried put the receiver to his ear.

"Hello, that you, chief?" came the voice from the other end.

"Yes," replied the chief.

"You know that woman you are looking for? I know where you can find her," said the informant.

"If you do, then tell me," demanded Chief Siegfried.

"Drive to the first filling station on Eighteenth street on the Kansas

"That's Kansas avenue," advised the chief.

"Yeah, out where the streets are torn up," the voice explained.

Chief Siegfried then demanded to know who the informer was.

"I haven't much time," came the reply and the connection was ended.

Left is a headline explaining that the Chief of Police received a phone call from an unknown person telling the police where Nell could be found.

Nell offered the $2,500 award for the arrest of 39 year-old Martin DePew, aka Marshall Deputy, the reputed kidnapping ringleader.

$2,500 REWARD
WANTED FOR KIDNAPPING

Reward will be paid for the *arrest and delivery* of this man in any jail in the United States, to an authorized Police Officer of Kansas City, Jackson County, Missouri.

William, Martin or Marshall Depew, alias Deputy, 37 years old, 6 ft tall, 190 to 200 lbs., brown hair, gray around temples; medium complexion, medium build, two or three upper teeth gold, small red mark on bridge near root of nose. Occupation: steam shovel operator and cement finisher, has been a R. R. fireman and brakeman on Eastern roads.

This man was a leader of a mob who kidnapped Mrs. Nellie Donnelly, of this city and held her for $75,000 ransom.

When arrested, hold and wire L. M. Siegfried, Chief of Police, Kansas City, Mo., and Officer will be sent with proper papers, at once.

Blanketing the entire country with fliers like that above, police sought the elusive Marshall Depew, wanted as the Donnelly kidnap leader. As we go to press, Depew is still at large. Watch for this badly wanted man.

Bottom left is the Kidnapping lair and the photo next to it is of the cots Nell and George were forced to lie upon.

The mug shot below is of 31 year-old Walter Werner, one of three men who abducted Nell.

Bottom right is a photo of DePew, a steam shovel operator.

To the upper right is Charles Mele, the man who beat and choked Nell in the backseat of the Lincoln causing her to bleed.

"THAT IS THE MAN."

Martin Depew, the target of a search by Kansas City police as the leader of the gang who kidnaped Mrs. Nell Donnelly last Wednesday and held her thirty-four hours in an isolated Wyandotte County farm cottage.

"That is he," Mrs. Donnelly said when the picture was shown her late yesterday. Her words were echoed, almost, by Paul Scheidt and William Lacy Browning, prisoners in the county jail, who confessed to their part in the kidnaping.

Depew was a steam shovel operator in his legitimate work. He is shown here beside the big scoop of a steam shovel belonging to the Marion Steam Shovel Company, 1231 Woodswether road.

MO. STATE PEN. 41716
Walter Werner

The Kidnapping

(Left to Right), Paul Scheidt and William L. Browning, arrested in connection with the kidnapping of Mrs. Nell Donnelly.

Calling all of the resources of his department into play, Lewis M. Siegfried, Kansas City police chief, together with his aids (shown herewith), pressed the hunt to a successful climax. Left to right: Chief Siegfried, Lieutenant Goodhue, Detective Rayen, George Blair, Mrs. Donnelly's chauffeur, and Detective Robeen.

Above is a photo of Paul Scheidt (on the left) with Lacy Browning next to him. Browning was contacted by DePew to find a hideout. Browning contacted Scheidt who was living at the farmhouse that was the kidnapping hideout. Scheidt was to receive $1,000 and Browning $5,000. Neither man saw any money for their troubles. Scheidt was acquitted and Browning served a short sentence for his involvement.

Top right is a picture of police officers who investigated Nell's kidnapping. With them is George Blair, Nell's chauffeur, virtually always referred to as the "negro chauffeur" in newspaper articles.

Right is the story how police traced DePew to South Africa where he was captured. DePew was a bigamist who left his second wife when she refused to enter Canada while DePew was on the run for kidnapping Nell.

THE INSIDE STORY OF THE DEPEW CAPTURE

By ERIC ROSENTHAL
Johannesburg, South Africa

The powerful influence of TRUE DETECTIVE MYSTERIES reaches ten thousand miles, and a notorious kidnapper finds himself in the grip of the Law. The capture stories of Taft Patton, murderer, and Henry Cooch, kidnapper, caught in the net of T.D.M.'s LINE-UP follow the DePew story

NELLY DON: A Stitch In Time

Far left shows the jury, Nell and Ethel DePew during the trial of Ethel Depew. Mrs. Depew had been a nurse the year before at the Donnelly home tending Paul. She was acquitted of any wrongdoing.

No money was ever paid, the gangsters found Nell before any transfers took place. Top center shows Kate McCormick Baty, Paul Donnelly (in chair), Mildred Frances and Lee Baty, Kate's husband reading about Nell's release after the kidnapping. Kate and Lee are the author/filmmaker's maternal grandparents.

Lower right shows a happy Nell glad to be home, but still shaken after the ordeal.

AS MRS. NELL Q. DONNELLY TELLS AGAIN THE STORY OF HER KIDNAPING, THE TRIAL OF MRS. ETHEL DEPEW.

THE JURY. (top)—Judge Ben Terte swore in the twelve men who will decide Mrs. Ethel Depew's fate. Rear row (left to right): Henry Ahern, 4024 Belleview avenue; Elmer Gurley, 2500 Harrison street; Frank D. Shrout, Grain Valley, Mo.; Claude L. Carpenter, 410 North Grand, Independence; Lowry Lane, Shi-a-Bar road and Eastman avenue; Harry A. Hurstis, 1300 Reservoir place. Front row (left to right): Delmar Sanders, 19 East Twenty-ninth street; Wilbur Ehret, 2741 Prospect avenue; Edward J. Kaufman, 812 Tracy avenue; Lloyd Spangler, 3324 Tracy avenue; E Le-Roy Cooper, 2241 Robert Gillham road; Lawrence P. Neff, 212 North Van Brunt boulevard.

THE KIDNAPING EVIDENCE ALL OVER AGAIN (center)—Mrs. Nell Q. Donnelly on the witness stand repeating once more the account of her abduction with her chauffeur December 16. Lawrence P. Neff, one of the jurors, is shown examining a ransom note.

THE ACCUSED (below)—Mrs. Ethel Depew listens attentively while Mrs. Donnelly recites the vivid details of the kidnaping. Mrs. Depew denies having any part in the kidnaping plot for which her husband, Martin Depew, faces life imprisonment. She was a nurse in the Donnelly home from Christmas to New Year's, 1930.

JOY REIGNED IN THE DONNELLY HOME AS HUSBAND AND RELATIVES READ OF FREEING OF MRS. DONNELLY BY KIDNAPERS.

When the second extra edition of The Times reached the Donnelly home early today Mrs. Donnelly already had sketched briefly the story of the kidnaping and gone to her room, but there was great interest in the detailed printed story, and, as shown above, four read the paper as one.

In the center seated and holding the paper is Paul Donnelly, husband of the kidnaped woman, who was tireless in his vigil, and who was eager at all times to pay the $75,000 demanded by the kidnapers as ransom. At his left is Miss Mildred Francis, his private secretary. The others are Mr. and Mrs. Lee Baty, Parsons, Kas. Mrs. Baty is a niece of Mrs. Donnelly. They came to Kansas City as soon as they learned of the kidnaping.

MRS. DONNELLY IS FOUND, SAFE

K.C. TIMES FRI-DEC 18-1931

The Garment Designer and Manufacturer Released Unharmed by the Kidnapers After 34 Hours in Captivity—Put Out of a Car Near the Sinclair Oil Refinery in Kansas City, Kansas—Blair, the Chauffeur, Also Is Released.

"THE $75,000 RANSOM IS NOT PAID"

The Victim of the Kidnapers Tells of Fighting Her Abductors When They Started to Put a Sack Over Her Head—"It Got My Irish Up."

Mrs. Nell Donnelly was found early this morning, unharmed.

They Walk Back.

The promised car did not appear. The chauffeur and Mrs. Donnelly had been freed of their blindfolds. They were on a street almost dark, the darkness pierced by dim street

Paid No Ransom, Reed Says.

Not one cent of ransom was paid to liberate Mrs. Nell Donnelly, Senator Reed said on her return.

"We did not arrange the matter with anyone," he said. "All we could do was to hope. It happened. That is all."

"Is this the car that came for me," she asked, from the sidewalk, apparently ready to dodge into the confectionary.

The officers showed their badges, and she went to the car. It was Mrs. Donnelly.

HAPPY TO BE HOME AGAIN.

Mrs. Nell Donnelly, at her home late yesterday, received flowers from friends who congratulated her upon her safe return, after being held thirty-four hours by kidnapers. Mrs. Donnelly has expressed a determination to give every aid to authorities in capturing her abductors. She is shown here beside a bouquet of roses, holding cards from friends.

How GANGSTERS Solved The DONNELLY KIDNAPING

By LEON N. HATFIELD

Held for staggering ransom and threatened with blindness, a beautiful Kansas City business woman faced a horrible fate.

Police were baffled by the clueless case.

Then gangland amazed the world by throwing its "gun squads" on the side of the law.

Here is the unbelievable story of how twenty-five carloads of underworld sleuths took the kidnap trail to solve the mystery.

A TELEPHONE bell rang as the curtain rose on Kansas City's greatest drama of 1931. Its musical chime stirred reverberating chords in a reception hall. A servant crossed noiselessly to answer the call, buy already a woman's voice is speaking on an extension line.

"Yes?"

A pause.

"Mr. Taylor is not at home. Is there a message?"

And then, after a few moments:

"I will let him know."

The first scene of the drama had been played but only a few of the actors realized the fact.

SOUGHT AS KIDNAP LEADER
Identified by his victim as the "brains" of the kidnaping band, Marshall (William or Martin) Depew, alias Deputy, was the subject of an intensive search as Kansas City detectives, aided by unofficial investigators in the underworld, scoured the midwest for the fugitive gang leader. In the picture, Depew is shown with his wife, a former nurse in the Donnelly home, who accompanied him on his flight.

Checkups on known criminals and scores of raids throughout Kansas City availed nothing in the Donnelly case until John Lazia, public-spirited citizen and prominent in political circles, offered to use his influence in organizing an unofficial search for the elusive abduction gang.

KIDNAPERS' RENDEZVOUS
Kidnaped as her car turned into the home driveway, Mrs. Donnelly was spirited away by the daring abductors to this rude dwelling, where she was threatened with loss of her eyesight if the ransom was not paid.

It was an hour or more later that night of December 16, when James E. Taylor, law partner of James A. Reed, former United States Senator, let himself in at the door of his comfortable home.

"You didn't stay long at the club," his wife greeted him as he laid aside his coat and hat.

"No. There didn't seem to be anything going on." "Someone called a while ago."

"Leave a message?"

"Yes. A man said, 'Please tell Mr. Taylor that if he goes to the Country Club Plaza he can get Mrs. Donnelly's car." Taylor laughed. "That's not for me. There's another James Taylor who has been helping in the drive for collection of motor car license fees. Someone is probably playing a joke on him. Mrs. Donnelly must have her licenses by this time"

Giving no more thought to the matter, Senator Reed's partner retired for the night.

On Opening his mail at the office next morning however, James R. Taylor scowled over sheets of scrawled writing he had just taken from their envelope.

Suddenly and the memory of that call sprang into his mind. He gripped a telephone and snapped out a number.

"Is Mrs. Donnelly th—— pped out. He listened for a moment.

—— l Mr. Donnelly that I must —— t once.

—— s rushing through a long

—— moned

—— capital, the illustrious —— A secretary appeared —— nded up to Reed. He

ABDUCTION VICTIM
Beautiful victim of a kidnap ring, Mrs. Neil Quinlan Donnelly, wealthy Kansas City manufacturer, found her life in jeopardy when newspapers blazoned the story of her abduction across their pages.

This is the April 1932 edition of Startling Detective. In those days, Detective Magazines served the function that "America's Most Wanted" and real crime programs do today, i.e., helping catch criminals.

A Kansas City Star sketch artist's rendition of the kidnapping ordeal.

KIDNAPED AT THE ENTRANCE TO THE DONNELLY HOME. A STRUGGLE IN THE CAR. WRITING NOTES BY FLASHLIGHT

PRISONERS IN A RURAL HIDE-OUT. LIBERATED IN THE EARLY DAWN AND A HAPPY ENDING...

Chapter Nine

Goodbye Paul Donnelly

On November 15, 1932, less than one year after being kidnapped, Nell divorced Paul Donnelly. They had personal assets of $1.27 million dollars. Nell bought Paul's interest in the Donnelly Garment Company for $1 million dollars and took complete control of the business. Fifty year-old Paul Donnelly was out.

On October 12, 1932, a month prior to the Donnelly divorce, 88 year-old Lura Reed died of pneumonia. In June of 1932, Reed's third attempt at a presidential nomination failed at the democratic convention in Chicago where Franklin Delano Roosevelt was nominated. Reed reportedly was offered the vice-presidency on the ticket, but declined stating he did not want a back seat on a hearse.

At a dinner party at Reed's home on December 13, 1933, Nell and her attorney again made national headlines when they asked their 20 guests to rise and be witness to their marriage performed by a federal judge. Most everybody present was surprised.

After the divorce, Paul Donnelly's life spiraled downward. He married a 23 year-old woman named Virginia George who was a college classmate of one of Nell's nieces. Paul financed Broadway plays starring his young wife. He squandered his fortune and became increasingly morose. On September 7, 1934, in Hartford, Connecticut, Paul, in a manic-depressed state hanged himself and died of strangulation suicide.

But life for Nell was only getting better. She had a child, a famous husband and a successful business to run which she did with a very kind heart.

Nell's marriage to Reed was a happy one. Reed formal-

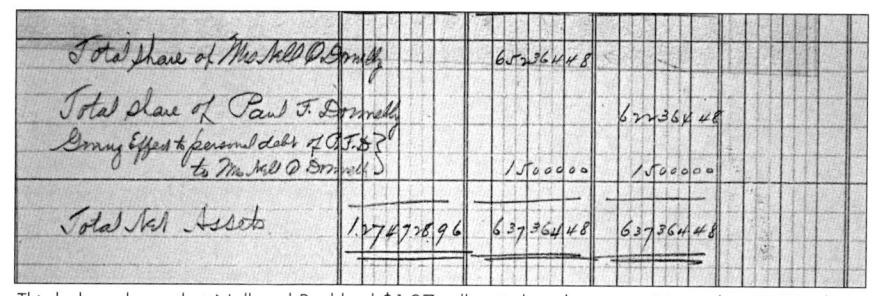

This ledger shows that Nell and Paul had $1.27 million in liquid assets in November 1932 when they were divorced. Nell bought Paul's interest in the Donnelly Garment Company for $1 million at the time of the divorce, terminating "A Modern Business Romance" after 26 years of marriage.

Above, Nell and Paul during happier times (c. 1927).

Right, Nell's divorce from Paul made headlines and so too would her marriage in another year.

MRS. NELL DONNELLY, KIDNAPERS' VICTIM, AWARDED DIVORCE

MRS. NELL DONNELLY.
By Associated Press.

KANSAS CITY, MO., November 15.—Mrs. Nell Quinlan Donnelly, wealthy garment manufacturer, who was the victim of a kidnaping plot last year which failed of its objective of $75,000 ransom, was granted a divorce late today from Paul Francis Donnelly.

Mrs. Donnelly said her husband had been absent from the family home, in front of which she was abducted last December, and that he had been guilty "of acts of cruelty and neglect."

Donnelly did not contest the suit.

Mrs. Donnelly was held prisoner more than thirty hours in a Wyandotte County, Kan., cottage, following her abduction, but was released voluntarily. Four of the kidnapers were given prison sentences.

ly adopted David and they called each other Partner. The couple bought a 7,000 acre ranch in north central Michigan and Reed taught Nell how to fish and hunt. They held huge venison dinners at the factory for the workers.

Lura and Jim Reed on board an ocean liner. Lura Reed died at age 88 in October 1932, one month before the Donnelly divorce.

Members of the Reed for President Bowling Team in 1932. Reed was nominated as a favorite son of Missouri and Tom Pendergast remained loyal to Reed, even though Reed had no chance of victory given the overwhelming support for FDR at the 1932 Democratic Convention in Chicago.

T. J. PENDERGAST'S LOYALTY TO REED HOLDS DELEGATES

His Pledged Word to Former Senator Is Being Kept to Letter.

By K. P. MIDDLETON
Of the Journal-Post Staff.

CHICAGO, June 28.—The strongly developed sense of political loyalty of a Kansas City Democratic leader stood forth Tuesday as an important factor in the slowing up of the Roosevelt nomination trend as the convention entered its second session.

The leader in question is T. J Pendergast. He had pledged his word long ago to be for James A.

Knowing full well Reed would not be the Democrats' choice for President, Pendergast nevertheless was steadfastly loyal to Reed in 1932.

Mr. James Alexander Reed
and
Mrs. Nell Quinlan Donnelly
announce their marriage
on Wednesday, the thirteenth of December
One thousand nine hundred and thirty-three
Kansas City, Missouri

Nell and Reed invited about 30 guests to a special holiday dinner on December 13, 1933. In attendance was a federal judge who upon cue asked everybody to rise and bear witness to the nuptials of Jim Reed and Nell Donnelly. It surprised everybody except for the author's Grandma, Kate McCormick Baty, who was Matron of Honor to Nell.

Newspaper photographers were on hand when Nell and Reed returned from their honeymoon and united with David, making for a very happy family. Reed was 72 years-old when he married 44 year-old Nell. Reed was 70 years-old when his son David was born.

Nell and David in Florida in 1933.

REED AND HIS BRIDE

James A. Reed, former United States senator from Missouri, and the former Mrs. Nell Donnelly, wealthy garment manufacturer, who were married recently at Kansas City. They are shown at the Reed home on New Year Day, where they held a reception for friends. Reed was attorney for Mrs. Donnelly at the time of her sensational kidnaping in 1931.

While Reed was the "Fighting Senator of Missouri" in public, his son David Reed remembers his dad as being a kind and gentle man. Reed and David called each other "Partner." No doubt David Reed was one of Jim Reed's proudest accomplishments so late in life.

Chapter Ten

Nell, the Beneficent Executive

By all accounts, Nell cared about her employees. She had the reputation of paying the highest wages in the field. She installed hardwood floors at the factory so her employees would not have to work on concrete all day. Free coffee and donuts greeted workers each morning. She subsidized a cafeteria so her workers could eat well but inexpensively. In the afternoon, workers were treated to free lemonade and snacks from a cart pushed around the floor.

Nell established a pension plan for her employees. She paid for any employee who wanted to go to college at night and established a scholarship fund for the children of her employees. There was a remnants store within the factory so workers could buy unused Nelly Don fabrics to make their own clothes. There was a slightly damaged dress store for the employees where they could buy Nelly Dons for pennies on the dollar.

Nell installed air conditioning as soon as it became available. On site was a medical clinic staffed full-time by two nurses and a doctor once a week who could write prescriptions. She paid for group hospitalization benefits. She paid for life insurance. There was a small grocery and butchery for employees to shop before heading home.

She bought a farm outside Kansas City where Nelly Don employees could go with their families to picnic, hike and fish. She bought a mansion in a Kansas City park and converted it to a recreation center where company parties were held or where any employee could reserve it for their own party. And party they did. They had dances, played sports and produced theatre together.

Nelly Don factory humming along in the mid-1930s.

Another booklet Nell published in 1936 celebrating the success and growth of Nelly Don. She liked to promote her company as family and in so doing inspired strong fealty by her employees.

Nelly Don Pioneers Luncheon recognizing long-time employees. Nell is seated in the second row, fifth from the right (1937).

Every Christmas Nell threw a party for families of her workers. Santa Claus delivered to each child a personalized gift he or she had requested.

Company parties and even athletics are fairly common in businesses today, but Nelly Don employees actually produced plays together as seen in the photograph below of the 1929 production of "Bashful Mr. Bobs."

Above is a photo of Nell, Kate McCormick Baty and Mary Kathryn Baty (O'Malley) in Miami, Florida, in 1933.

GOOD HEALTH

(Left) • A full-time trained nurse in her dispensary to safeguard the health of every employee . . . a personal service in the Nelly Don manner.

PARTIES

(Right) • The annual Christmas Party for the employees and their kiddies finds Nelly Don the hostess.

GOOD FOOD

(Right) • Piping hot or ice-chilled, Winter or Summer, there's the sunny cafeteria for a well-balanced, inexpensive diet.

Page Fourteen

GOOD FUN

(Left) • The Athletic Association furnishes lots of fun—a play or a carnival for every one.

Page Fifteen

NOVEMBER 12, 1937.
Donnelly Employes Get Clubhouse

Employes of the Donnelly Garment company have a clubhouse with spacious grounds for their recreation. It was purchased for their use by Mrs. James A. Reed, head of the company. A view of the recreation center near Sixty-third street and Swope parkway is shown.

'CLUB HOUSE' IS GIVEN EMPLOYES OF GARMENT CO.

Mrs. Nell Donnelly Reed Renovates Home as Recreation Spot.

Employes of the Donnelly Garment company now have a recreation center at which they may enjoy their days of leisure and evenings in an atmosphere somewhat similar to that of a country club.

The center is on a 5-acre tract on the south side of Sixty-third street, just east of Swope parkway. The huge stone house was the home of the late Edward E. Yates, widely known Kansas City attorney.

Mrs. James A. Reed, head of the garment company, purchased the property several months ago from the Yates estate. Several weeks were required to get the ground into shape and redecorate the house. That was completed about three weeks ago and a housewarming followed.

Ovens were built on the grounds and comfortable furniture was installed in the house.

"The project was planned and completed for the comfort and entertainment of my employes," Mrs. Reed said today.

She explained that the house was rearranged to permit private parties for small groups of her employes. It also has a dance floor, reading room and other entertainment features. While the recreation house will accomodate only about 100 at a time, the grounds are spacious enough, she said, to care for her entire working force of more than 1,000.

"And Swope park adjoins the grounds, so they should have plenty of room," she said.

Mr. Yates, who died several years ago, was once a law partner of Mrs. Reed's husband.

Nell purchased a clubhouse in Kansas City for company parties and for a place for employees to host their own parties at no cost. Nell also purchased a farm outside Kansas City for employees to picnic and recreate.

Above is Nell at one of her many huge Christmas parties for the children of her workers.

Below is a photo of the infirmary on-site at the Nelly Don plant (c. 1936).

Nell spent lavishly on the children of her workers at Christmastime throwing huge parties where each child received the gift from Santa Claus he or she requested, like dolls, bicycles, sleds and other big ticket items.

Below right are Baty, Glynn and O'Malley children, all first cousins of one another with Santa Claus and Lee and Kate McCormick Baty.

Lower left, in March 1931, using his powerful oratorical skills, Reed successfully defended accused murderer Myrtle Bennett who shot her husband over a hand of Bridge in front of several eyewitnesses. Mrs. Bennett testified that the gun's firing was accidental, even though it discharged four rounds. Reed's victory in the face of certain defeat enhanced his national reputation as a great trial attorney.

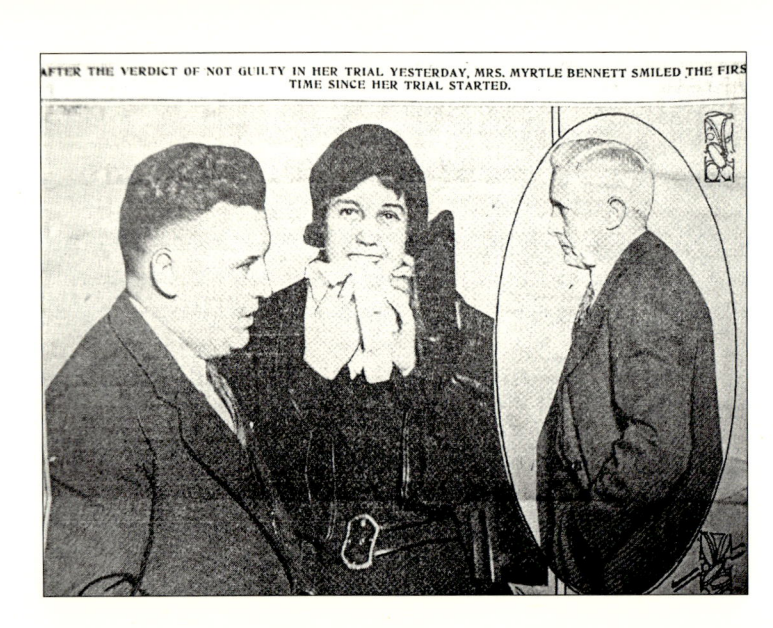

Chapter Eleven

Union Target: Nelly Don

Even in retirement, Reed remained vocal politically and sharply criticized FDR's New Deal Policies and campaigned against his re-election in 1936 and 1940.

As a result, the International Ladies Garment Workers Union declared war against the Donnelly Garment Company, and in 1937 allocated $100,000 to unionize what was by then the largest dress manufacturing company in the United States. The ILGWU's leader, David Dubinsky, charged that Nelly Don exploited its workers, thereby undermining the entire women's garment industry and that the ILGWU would not rest until Nelly Don was unionized.

Nell disliked and distrusted unions. She believed she treated her workers better than if they belonged to a union. Picketers for the national union appeared outside her plant and workers were harassed and incidents of violence were reported. In defiance of the national union and of their own accord, Nell's employees drafted a loyalty declaration professing their confidence in Nell rather than "outside agitators." Nell took great pride in knowing that all but six of more than 1,300 workers signed the loyalty declaration.

Nell's workers voted against joining the ILGWU and instead formed the Donnelly Garment Company Worker's Union. But the FDR-stacked National Labor Relations Board ordered Nell to cut all ties with the independent union formed by her workers, refund dues and pledge to engage in what the Board termed "fair labor practices."

Reed immediately attacked the order alleging bias and prejudice by the Board and removed the matter to federal court where lawyers litigated the case for seven years

---

Garment Union Votes War on James A. Reed

Cites Ex-Senator, Whose Wife Runs Factory, in Unionization Campaign

Gives $100,000 for Drive

Dubinsky Says He'll Teach Him 'Real Americanism'

Special to the Herald Tribune

ATLANTIC CITY, May 10.—Celebrating a victory in Montreal, where unionization has been considered "impossible," the International Ladies' Garment Workers' Union moved today to organize needleworkers in New England, Philadelphia, Cleveland and Kansas City.

The twenty-third convention, beginning its second week here in the Hotel Chelsea, voted $100,000 for the

Herald Tribune photo—Acme
Mrs. James A. Reed

Her Factory Union Target

In the top article, the "Real Americanism" reference is a rejoinder from the president of the ILGWU David Dubinsky, a Russian emigrant who became a naturalized U.S. citizen. Dubinsky argued that unionism was democratic and patriotic. Reed questioned whether Dubinsky could understand America given his socialistic upbringing.

WHO WANTS TO BE A MEMBER OF A SCAB UNION?

★ ★ ★

Donnelly Garment Company Violates Wagner Labor Act. Organizes Company Union and All Workers Are Forced to Pay Tribute to a Lawyer for Violating the Law

★ ★ ★

To mislead the workers of the Donnelly Garment Company, the executives of the firm have decided to impose a company union upon the workers and continue in the shop the inhuman speed-up system, long hours and low wages.

For $500 that a certain lawyer has already received, the spies, who are on the payroll of the strike-breaking agency employed by the Donnelly Garment Company, have organized this company

The pamphlet left was distributed by the ILGWU and excoriated Nelly Don for its obstinate opposition to joining ranks with the national union. One argument was that by not unionizing, Nelly Don was causing harm to other garment workers around the country because the union needed Nelly Don, America's largest dressmaker, to grow its power.

before the 8th Circuit U.S. Court of Appeals sustained the right of the Donnelly Garment Company to have its own union and for the ILGWU to stop picketing the company and stop circulating false and libelous pamphlets about the company. Nell won, of course, because she's Nell.

Reed Says Garment Union Attempting To Punish Him For Opposing FDR In 1936

Right, ILGWU president David Dubinsky.

Headlines: Reed blamed FDR for the union's aggressive targeting of Nelly Don and went on to accuse ILGWU's leaders as being "Red," i.e., communists.

Top right, a mass meeting of 1,300 Nelly Don workers to vote against the ILGWU.

Far right, James A. Reed versus Frank P. Walsh was a clash of legal titans. Walsh and Reed had a long history and literally would not speak to one another, such was their enmity.

Nell beams with pride as she is presented a "loyalty oath" from her workers rejecting "outside agitators."

—Kansas City Star Photograph.
THREE WOMEN EMPLOYEES OF THE DONNELLY GARMENT COMPANY, WHO CIRCULATED A PRONOUNCEMENT OF LOYALTY TO MRS. JAMES A. REED, HEAD OF THE CONCERN, ARE SHOWN AS THEY GAVE THE SIGNATURE-FILLED SHEETS TO MRS. REED. FROM LEFT TO RIGHT, THOSE SHOWN IN THE PICTURE ARE MRS. PAULINE SHARTZER, 3620 MERSINGTON AVENUE; MRS. INEZ WARREN, 4114 EAST ELEVENTH STREET; MRS. MARY SPROFERA, 5013 TROOST AVENUE, AND MRS. REED.

REED STAMPS 'RED' BRAND ON UNION LEADERS

Former Senator Also Puts 'Racketeer' Label on Court Opponents.

BRIEFS WILL BE FILED

Donnelly Injunction Suit Hearing Comes to End in Federal Court.

Reed and Walsh, Political Foes, Speak for First Time in 5 Years

JAMES A. REED.   FRANK P. WALSH.

By the Associated Press.
KANSAS CITY, Nov. 6.—Frank P. Walsh, New York lawyer, and former senator James A. Reed of Missouri split over the New Deal five years ago and haven't been speaking since.
But they broke the silence yesterday. Walsh is here to defend the International Ladies' Garment Workers' Union in an injunction suit brought by the Donnelly Garment Co., for which Reed is attorney.
Reed was examining a witness when Walsh interrupted.
"Let her go ahead and talk," Reed snapped.
Walsh bowed. "I thank you for speaking to me," he said.
"That's under pressure," Reed replied, and turned away.

Chapter Twelve

Nelly Don Goes to War

Rosie the Riveter meet Nelly Don! Not only did Nell manufacture uniforms for American armed-services women, but she designed heavy-industry work clothes using live models to make the garments as comfortable as possible.

They had specially cut sleeves, non-binding shoulders, easily accessible pockets and were "generously cut to eliminate strain from action." The blouses, slacks, coveralls and aprons were easy to wash and treated to resist wrinkling.

Nell marketed directly to wartime industries such as oil processing, gunpowder manufacturing and airplane assembly. She opened up a second plant in St. Joseph, Missouri, dedicated solely to the manufacture of wartime apparel. It is said that Nell made 5 million pairs of G.I. underwear.

But Nell was no war profiteer. Throughout WWII, Nell charged no more than what it cost to make the clothing, enjoying no significant profit. Further, her plants (using the now-famous Nelly Don sectionalized method of production) were tailor-made to produce quickly mass quantities of uniforms and work clothes.

Nell was a true civilian patriot and understood the important impact she had on ensuring American victory. In recognition of her company's efforts, the U.S. Government bestowed on the Donnelly Garment Company two Army/Navy "E for Excellence Awards," a proud achievement for the entire "Nelly Don Family" as Nell affectionately referenced her company.

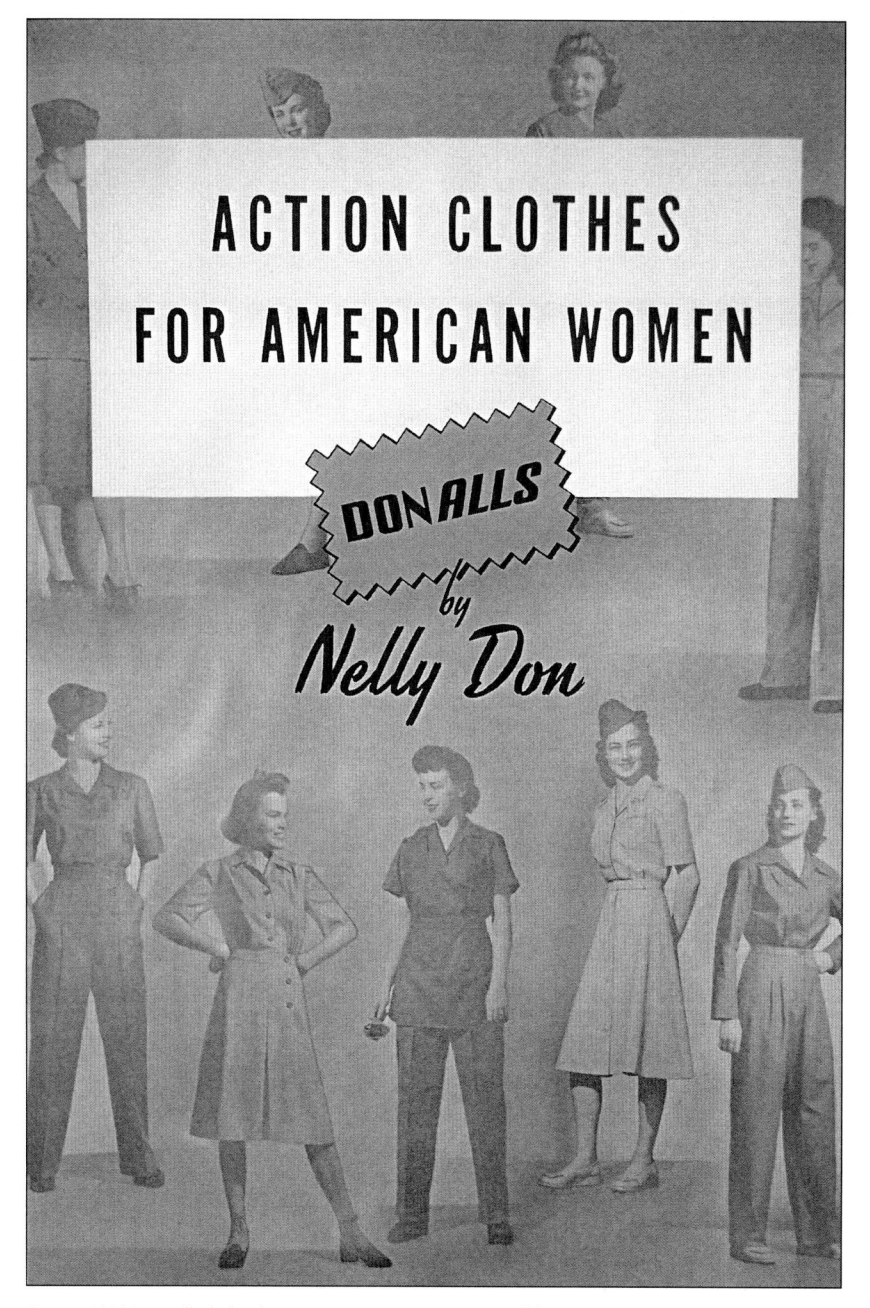

During WWII, Nell clothed American service women and those women who replaced men in heavy industries.

"We know that a well-dressed worker, consciously satisfied with her appearance, will be the most efficient."

Nelly Don

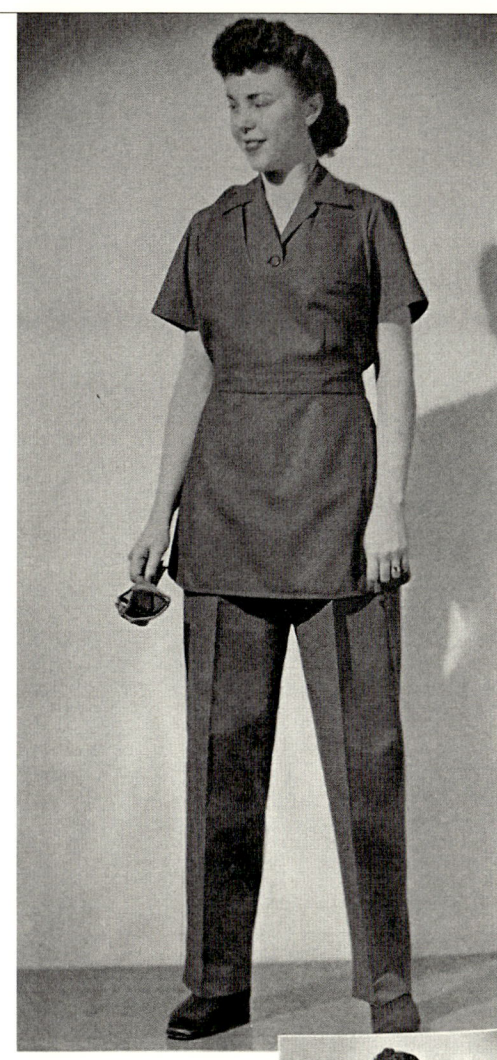

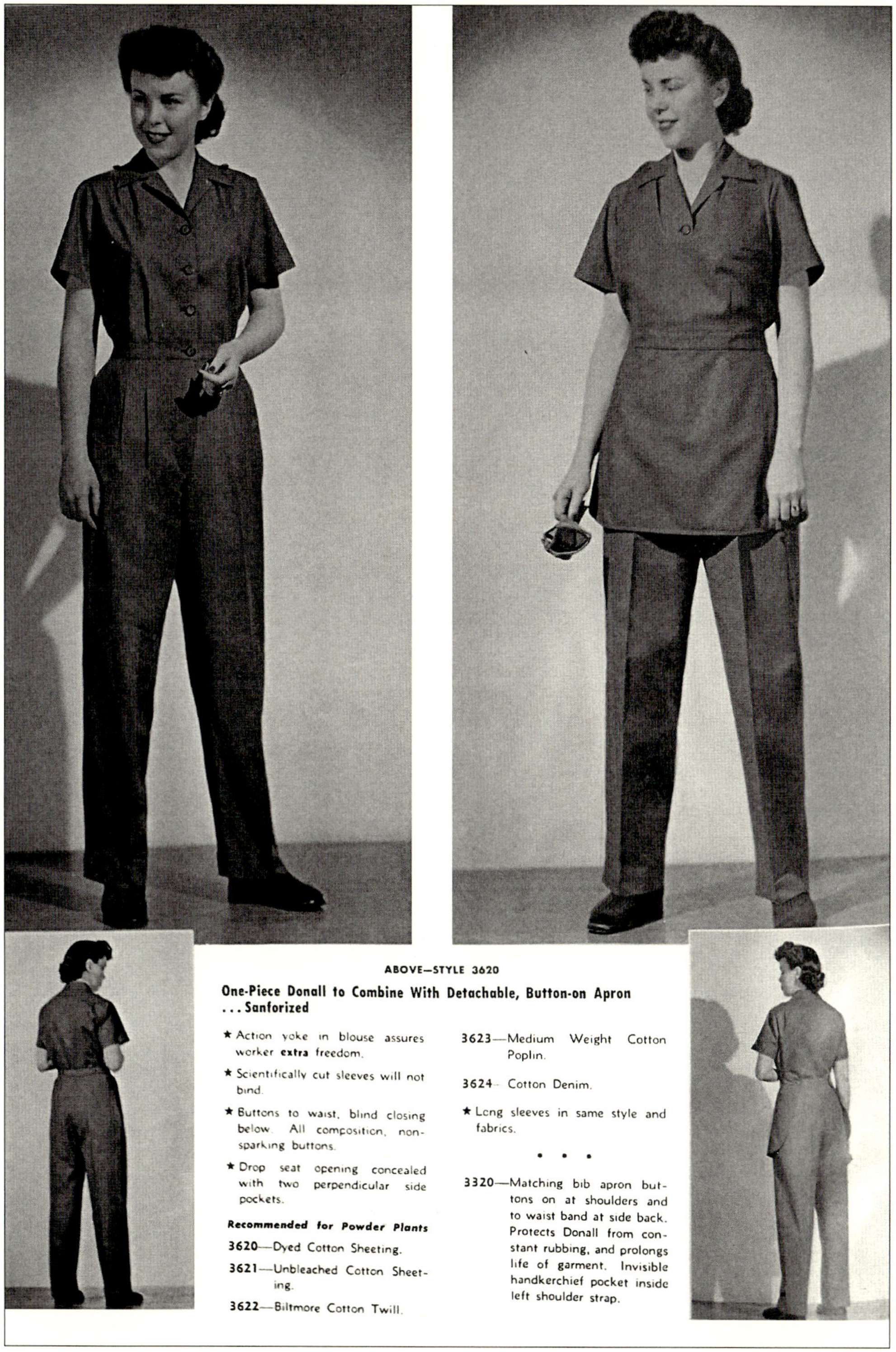

Nelly Don Goes to War

ABOVE—STYLE 3620
One-Piece Donall to Combine With Detachable, Button-on Apron ... Sanforized

★ Action yoke in blouse assures worker **extra** freedom.

★ Scientifically cut sleeves will not bind.

★ Buttons to waist, blind closing below. All composition, non-sparking buttons.

★ Drop seat opening concealed with two perpendicular side pockets.

Recommended for Powder Plants

3620—Dyed Cotton Sheeting.
3621—Unbleached Cotton Sheeting.
3622—Biltmore Cotton Twill.
3623—Medium Weight Cotton Poplin.
3624—Cotton Denim.

★ Long sleeves in same style and fabrics.

• • •

3320—Matching bib apron buttons on at shoulders and to waist band at side back. Protects Donall from constant rubbing, and prolongs life of garment. Invisible handkerchief pocket inside left shoulder strap.

"Women who enjoy the fit, color and style of garment they are wearing can give all of their attention to work."

Nelly Don

NELLY DON: A Stitch In Time

Nell liked IKE as both a general and president and it was during the Eisenhower presidency and after Reed's death that Nell switched to the Republican Party.

Nelly Don Goes to War

Reed with Nell in his Golden Years, the early 1940s. They spent much time at the Reed Ranch in Michigan. Reed saw David grow to be 13 years old.

On September 8, 1944, following a bout of bronchitis, 82 year-old Senator James A. Reed died at the ranch in Michigan. Invariably he was described as the fighting senator from Missouri. He believed that dissent was a necessary ingredient of democracy, and that even if a majority of people disagreed with him, he was not necessarily wrong.

Nell would never remarry, but instead proudly wore the moniker Mrs. James A. Reed for the rest of her life. She often counted the eleven years married to Jim Reed as the happiest of her life.

Chapter Thirteen

Nelly Don at its Zenith!

By 1947, Nelly Don was posting $14 million in annual sales during a period when New York manufacturers considered themselves lucky if they made $6 million dollars. Nelly Don was the largest company of its kind in the world.

Nell then set off on her most ambitious plan yet, to build the single largest dress manufacturing plant on the face of the planet, sprawling two city blocks encompassing more than 206,000 square feet. It was a marvel of efficiency and the company continued to thrive.

The building housed a completely equipped restaurant, eight large rest rooms and a company store stocking meat and farm products for employees. Fabrics were delivered via a railroad spur and proceeded on a north-to-south route from yard goods to finished dresses. Electric ceiling fans circulated the air, changing it completely every three to six minutes. The windows extended from floor to ceiling lining the east and west walls. They were heat resistant and tinted light blue to soften the glare of the sun. A skylight extended the entire length of the building adding brilliance to the fluorescent lighting.

Sewing machines were grouped in sections, each section being a miniature factory in itself and engineered to turn out one type of garment in bulk.

From 1947 until nine years later when Nell sold her interest in the Donnelly Garment Company, Nelly Don clothed more women than any other company. She was the *grande dame* of the garment industry.

Fashion Topix magazine covered the opening of the new Nelly Don plant in 1947, the largest dress manufacturing building in the world at that time. It was designed to improve output while sustaining quality.

"At the end of production, the Nelly Don dresses are expertly tissue-wrapped and proceed to the shipping department. And very promptly these dresses, signed by the lady from Missouri, will arrive fresh and clean in stores from Providence to Walla Walla, from the Phillipines to African Egypt."

Nelly Don at its Zenith! 77

From the House of Nelly Don

Above is the Corrigan Building where Nell had her factory from 1928 to 1947. It is on the National Registry of Historic Sites.

Above right, Anna Ruth and Helen Donnelly, Paul's sisters standing in front of the house where Nelly Don started at 31st & Montgall in Kansas City, MO (c. 1916).

Right is what originally was known as the Coca-Cola Building in KC, is now called the Western Auto Building and has been converted to upscale condominiums. The Nelly Don plant was housed there from about 1920 to 1928.

Top Left is a national ad showing Kansas City, Missouri, as a major player in garment manufacturing.

Right is a portrait photograph of Nell c. 1940.

Nelly Don at its Zenith! 79

Top left is the last of the print set "Nelly Don American Fashions."

Above is an oil portrait of Nell presented to her by her employees upon the opening of the new factory in 1947.

Left is the cover of the advertising circular Nell used to promote Nelly Don and its humongous factory.

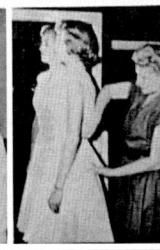

Laura Skinner Baty, Nell, David, Eddie Baty (c. 1950).

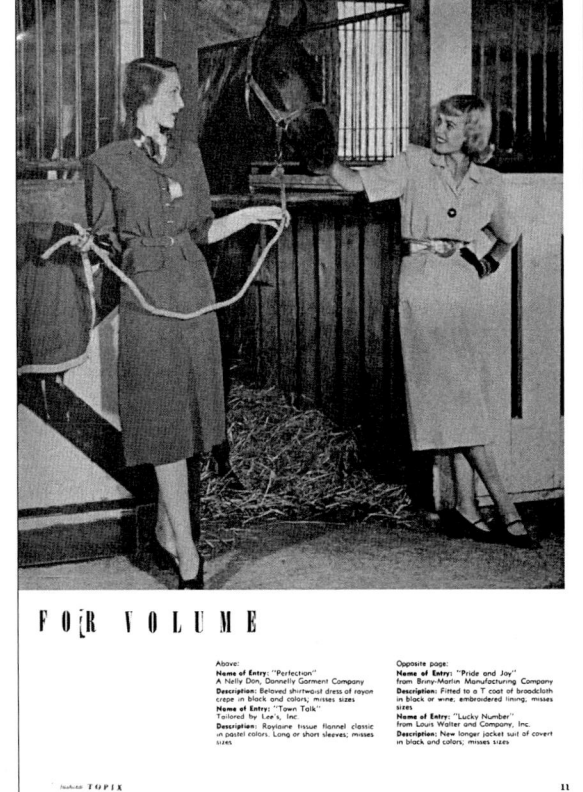

Various Nelly Don ads and circulars.

In the top left image, the woman sitting by herself is Katie Schleicher, the first employee for Nelly Don who was a neighbor of Nell's when the company began in 1916.

The bottom right photo is Lee Baty who ran production at Nelly Don for nearly 30 years and is the author's grandfather. Men were a definite minority at Nelly Don, but Lee Baty seems quite content nonetheless.

Nelly Don at its Zenith!

Far left, Nell in a full-length fashion portrait (c. 1947), when Nell was in her mid-to-late 50s.

The styles are definitely changing as fashions move into the 1950s.

NELLY DON RADIO SPOT ANNOUNCEMENTS

Spring-and-Resort, 1953

NELLY DON SPRING WARDROBE IDEAS

Here's fresh fashion news from STORE NAME'S NELLY DON Department! The new Spring-and-Resort Collection by NELLY DON has just arrived with enough wonderful wardrobe ideas to take you from here through spring. You'll find dresses and suits in cottons, silk, rayon, nylon, linen - clothes that look smart from coffee to curfew. And NELLY DON, you know, is the designer who believes that every woman can look like a million without spending one. So her excellent clothes with all their fine little dressmaker touches are always sensibly priced. Come to STORE NAME'S NELLY DON Shop and choose your spring wardrobe from our varied collection. Stop in today and "Just Try One On".

NELLY DON FAIRWEATHER SUITS

What could be smarter for the South, or for spring in town than a really well-cut suit? Perhaps you'll take yours in cotton, or one of the new soft "wonder fabrics", or perhaps you're looking for a smart little silk suit as a wardrobe mainstay. In any event, STORE NAME'S NELLY DON Shop is the place for you! Here you'll find NELLY DON'S newest collection of Fairweather suits, famous for their excellent tailored lines, their beautiful fit - and their sensible prices. Look for NELLY DON'S double-breasted suit of imported Doupioni silk shantung featured in January Charm - or better still, come to STORE NAME'S NELLY DON Shop soon and see them all.

Nelly Don prepared radio spots for retailers to use on the air.

Nelly Don at its Zenith!

Top left, a skipper middy dress.

Top right, the easy overblouse dress, the "best look a two-piecer can have."

Standing left model, a seersucker sheath dress, lean and easy cut.

Below, "elegant simplicity, a wear everywhere" dress.

Nell enjoyed wordplay, as in this 1941 circular.

Nelly Don model Lila Leeds' career goes up in smoke!

One particular story that caught our attention surrounds this young model, her name was Lila Leeds, who at some point after modeling for Nelly Don headed west to find fame and fortune in Hollywood where her good looks garnered studio attention. She acted in several B movies and appeared to have a promising career. But then she and another girlfriend hooked up with actor Robert Mitchum in 1949 and were at Mitchum's home in the Hollywood Hills when they were arrested for smoking marijuana. The studio had too much invested in Mitchum to let this scandal ruin his career, but Lila Leeds was expendable. She ended up being convicted and banished from the State of California. She battled drug addiction and had several failed marriages and died in relative obscurity.

Lila and actor Robert Mitchum (second from right) being sentenced to 60 days on narcotics charges in 1949. With them are their lawyers, Grant Cooper (beside her) and Jerry Geisler.

Chapter Fourteen

Nell Devotes Herself to Altruism

Throughout her life, Nell remembered those people and institutions that helped her along the way. She established the Nelly Don awards at Lindenwood College recognizing students in the home economics department for outstanding dress designs. She also endowed a specialized computer course in the mathematics department. In 1949, Nell received an honorary degree of doctor of laws from Lindenwood College, and in 1952 Coe College, the school Jim Reed quit to support his family, awarded Nell an honorary doctor of humanities degree.

In 1956, sensing changes in the fashion industry, Nell sold the Donnelly Garment Company. It had been 40 years since she had first sewn that pink gingham check frock that was so wildly popular.

Nell spent time with family, became a noted philanthropist and served on boards and commissions. In 1977, she was recognized as the National Republican Woman of the Year.

She remained an avid outdoors woman. She donated 840 acres of land outside Kansas City establishing the James A. Reed Wildlife Area for hunting and fishing.

Nell made good on a promise to herself around the time of the kidnapping, and that was to employ George Blair for the rest of his life. For 48 years, George Seaton Blair remained Nell's chauffeur, butler and loyal confidante. George, who grew up picking cotton around Charleston, Arkansas, was ninth of 12 siblings whose parents were devout Methodists and who grew cotton as sharecroppers. George died of a heart attack at the ranch in Michigan in 1977. David Reed, Nell's son wrote:

Continued on Page 90

Left, Nell with R. Crosby Kemper. When he founded his own bank, Nell named him trustee of her fortune.

Bottom, Nell with Sen. Barry Goldwater, 1964 GOP presidential candidate.

THE JAMES A. REED AREA

THE MISSOURI CONSERVATION COMMISSION

Frank P. Briggs, Macon; Ted Butler, Bennett Spring; Ben Cash, Kennett; Dru L. Pippin, Waynesville

The James A. Reed Memorial Wildlife Area is designed primarily as a public fishing area, but other wildlife and public use has been planned. The Conservation Commission has constructed six small fishing lakes on the area, with a total of 129 acres. It has also put into effect a comprehensive program for improving upland game habitat, to increase quail and rabbits. Limited rabbit hunting is permitted on the Reed Area, and field trials are major events. Provisions have been made for field archery, nature study and other uses.

The area came into being in July, 1952, when Mrs. Reed made a gift of land to the Conservation Commission as a memorial to her husband, the late Senator James A. Reed, with the stipulation that the Commission purchase enough additional land to make a workable unit. The land was acquired by the Commission in parcels and to date totals 1,971 acres. Besides headquarters and service buildings, there are two dwellings for resident area personnel. Access roads and ample parking facilities have also been constructed.

The James A. Reed Memorial Wildlife Area is advantageously located, close to Missouri's second largest metropolitan area. It is expected to be extremely popular with sportsmen, who will long enjoy this tangible evidence of public-spirited generosity on the part of Mrs. Reed. It is a living memorial to an eminent Missourian, and a welcome gift to the people of Missouri.

Nell donated most of the land to establish the James A. Reed Wildlife Area outside Kansas City. A bronze plaque memorializes Reed and Lake Nell is named in her honor. The area is open to the public for hunting, fishing and other recreational activities.

Nell Devotes Herself to Altruism

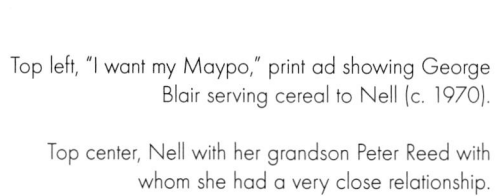

87

Top left, "I want my Maypo," print ad showing George Blair serving cereal to Nell (c. 1970).

Top center, Nell with her grandson Peter Reed with whom she had a very close relationship.

Top right, photo of Nell and George celebrating 40 years together.

Right, Nell receiving honors at the 1976 National Republican Convention in Kansas City as GOP Woman of the Year.

NELLY DON: A Stitch In Time

Top left, Nell with Missouri Senator Kit Bond (c. 1976)

Top right, Nell with grandson James A. Reed II at the ranch in Michigan (c. 1976)

Bottom left, Nell often made the society pages in Kansas City during her post-Nelly Don years.

Bottom right, George Blair's family with George as a little boy standing in the middle behind his sister in the white dress (c. 1907). His parents were cotton sharecroppers in Arkansas.

JOINT hostesses, Mrs. James A. Reed and her sister-in-law, Mrs. John A. Reed (far right) are shown with Mrs. James Preston Kem (center) at Mission Hills Country Club. The occasion was a beautiful autumn luncheon on September 28, which honored Mrs. Kem of Washington, D.C., the wife of Missouri's Senator Kem.

THE INDEPENDENT is a weekly magazine of distinguished society, chronicling club, sports and cultural events, with a complete coverage in Kansas City's preferred buyers' market. Its subscriptions extend to cosmopolitan areas throughout the United States and cover the foreign fields from Denmark to Honolulu. Published by the Creel Publishing Company, Kansas City, Missouri, and entered as Second-Class Matter at the Postoffice at Kansas City, Missouri, under the Act of Congress, March 3, 1899. Communications intended for publication must be received at the office not later than Friday of week preceding date of publication. Unsolicited manuscripts will not be returned. Advertising rates upon application. Subscription Rates: Year $3.50. Foreign Countries, Year $4.50; Canada, Year $4.00. Single copies 20 cents.

Nell Devotes Herself to Altruism

Top left, Nell and David Reed (center seated) at a family gathering of George Blair. Because George displayed such bravery and stoicism during the kidnapping, Nell promised herself that if they survived the ordeal that she would employ George Blair the rest of his life, which she did.

Seven point buck pole trophy finds Mrs. James Reed among the lucky hunters

A tea last Sunday at the residence of Mrs. James A. Reed was the starting point for a concert to be given by Lillian Murphy, proceeds to go to the rising young soprano and to the Philharmonic: Seated, l. to r., Mrs. Henry L. McCune, Mrs. Reed, Mrs. John R. Keach; standing, l. to r., Mrs. Burnham Hockaday, Mrs. Alfred B. Egan and Mrs. Charles M. Bush.

Bottom left is a young George Blair with his wife Savannah seated in the dark dress in front of him and his sister Hazel Anderson who provided this photo (c. 1935).

Bottom center is a photo from The Independent, a popular society magazine in Kansas City.

Far right, in 1981 at the age of 92, Nell shot the first buck of the Michigan deer season.

Nell Donnelly Reed is dead at age 102

Kansas City's 'grand lady of the garment industry' was business leader for decades.

By AMY SNIDER
Staff Writer

After a whirlwind century of life marked by success, romance and politics, Nell Donnelly Reed died quietly Sunday morning in her Kansas City home.

She was 102 years old.

Reed, often called the "grand lady of the garment industry," married U.S. Sen. James A. Reed in 1933, but she was perhaps best known for the changes she wrought in the women's ready-to-wear clothing industry in the 1920s.

The Kansas City woman built her home dress-making avocation into what became the multimillion-dollar Nelly Don Inc. garment company.

"She was very proud of her business," said her son, David Q. Reed of Kansas City. "She would tell stories."

He said his mother, who had been ill for several years, outlived almost all her contemporaries. "The old friends have been falling like the leaves in autumn," he said.

Born Ellen Quinlan on March 6, 1889, Reed grew up in Parsons, Kan., where her father moved from County Cork, Ireland, to work for the railroad.

She was the twelfth of 13 children in her family.

She moved to Kansas City as the child bride of Paul F. Donnelly, a credit man for a shoe company. Then in 1916, her career in the garment business blossomed.

Legend has it that the young bride had rebelled against the shapeless, frumpy housedresses of the era. So Nell Donnelly Reed, wanting to look pretty for her husband, stitched up some ruffled clothes for herself.

After receiving compliments

See **NELL, A-9, Col. 1**

Nell Donnelly Reed, pictured in a 1978 photograph, once summed up her business success by saying, "I just did what came naturally."

Nell Quinlan Donnelly Reed lived the last 30 years of her life at the famed Walnuts Apartments in Kansas City just south of the Country Club Plaza. Perhaps more than any other single person, Nell influenced the fashion of women in America during the 20th century.

David Reed Family – back row standing left to right, John, Peter and James A. Reed II. Front row left to right, Tinker, Ellen and David Reed (c. 1973).

Continued from Page 85

"George Blair was my oldest friend. One of my earliest memories was looking up from where a little boy looks up, at his smiling, kindly face. He helped me in all the little ways a little boy needs help and I loved him."

After Nell sold the Donnelly Garment Company in 1956, the new owners promptly changed its name to Nelly Don. It fared well through most of the 1960s and in 1968 finally affiliated with the International Ladies Garment Workers Union.

In the early 1970s, the company began selling fabric by the yard, something Nell had always disfavored because it took sales away from ready-made dresses. The "fabric-by-the-yard" idea failed, taking a great American company down. In May 1978, the Nelly Don company filed for bankruptcy and today is out of business.

Nell remained irrepressible. In 1981, at the age of 92, she shot the first buck of the Michigan deer season.

She was heralded as the grand lady of the garment industry, a gentle lady tycoon. She proudly defended the memory of her second husband James A. Reed.

Providence seems to have connected Nell with Reed. On September 8, 1991, Nell died peacefully in her home, 47 years to the day that Reed died. She was 102 years old and had outlived all twelve of her brothers and sisters.

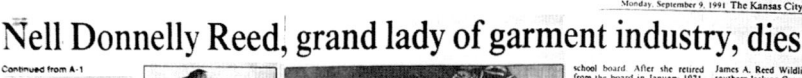

Monday, September 9, 1991 The Kansas City Star A-9

Nell Donnelly Reed, grand lady of garment industry, dies